Play

CATHERINE & LOREN
BROADUS

WORD BOOKS
PUBLISHER
WACO, TEXAS

A DIVISION OF
WORD, INCORPORATED

PLAY—IT'S NOT JUST FOR KIDS

Library of Congress Cataloging in Publication Data

Broadus, Catherine.
Play—it's not just for kids.

1. Leisure—Psychological aspects. 2. Play—Psychological aspects. 3. Play—Religious aspects. I. Broadus, Loren. II. Title.
GV14.4.B76 1987 790′.01′32 86–32594
ISBN 0–8499–3080–4

Printed in the United States of America

7898 FG 987654321

Dedicated to

Ellis Yonge and *Sid Hale*

Two of the best players and people the authors have ever known

Acknowledgments

The Board of Trustees, faculty, staff, and students of Lexington Theological Seminary supported the authors in the writing of this book. The Board granted Loren a sabbatical year to research, write, and "play" with the subject. The faculty not only recommended the sabbatical plan, they, the staff, and students helped with the research, offering suggestions, enduring interviews, and filling out questionnaires. Hundreds of people filled out questionnaires and granted interviews, and scores of people took the time to write lengthy letters describing their ideas about and practices of play and worship.

Walter Johnson read the manuscript and offered suggestions for improving it. Susan Lange patiently read a handwritten copy, corrected obvious errors, and typed the manuscript.

The authors appreciate very much the assistance of all these people in the production of *Play—It's Not Just for Kids.*

Contents

Introduction

Novelist and essayist E. B. White observed, "If the world were merely seductive that would be easy. If it were merely challenging, that would not be a problem, but I rise in the morning torn between a desire to improve (or save) the world and a desire to enjoy (or savor) the world. This makes it hard to plan the day."[1]

This book contends that what appears to be a dilemma for E. B. White and others is not an either/or issue. Instead, we are created both to "save" and to enjoy the world, to work and to play, to think and to feel, to live the rhythm of life, and to enjoy it most of the time.

In preparation for writing *How to Stop Procrastinating and Start Living,* Loren discovered that most people who are not organized personally, and many who are masters of efficiency, are not enjoying their work or play. If you are one of these people, this book could help you reverse the trend and start looking forward to Monday's work and Saturday's play. It could help you use the rhythm of life to keep your interest and energy high and your blood pressure low.

Because play and personal renewal are not simple

problems to be solved intellectually by Aristotelian logic—but a complex phenomenon that involves thoughts, feelings, and behavior—the material in this book engages both the mind and the emotions. Each chapter strives to help you reflect on your experiences, to examine your attitudes and if necessary, to develop an approach to life that will reduce unnecessary stress, increase your satisfaction in who you are becoming, and enable you to celebrate God's creative nature in you, others, and the world.

PLAY—It's Not Just for Kids is not just a catchy title, it is a fact of life. People who do not play playfully (play "for their lives") suffer physical, emotional, and spiritual death.

An editorial note: Except in direct quotes from other authors, inclusive language is used. Catherine and Loren played with the idea of including brackets in quotes [her], [she], [female], and so on, but abandoned the thought when too many brackets began to distract from ideas.

Play with this book and have fun doing it.

Play

1

Play for Your Life

In *God Is No Fool,* Lois Cheney describes this familiar incident.[1]

Once, on a week day, I was spending some hours at the beach and I saw a mother and her little boy. The day was perfect—bright and warm. The beach was quiet and there were very few people there. In quiet little clusters they sunned and slept and read and swam lazily. All was quite different from the weekend water riot of noise, music, and shouting.

The white, white skin of both the mother and the boy told quite clearly that this was not a frequent type of outing for them. I watched the boy as he shed the tightness and duty and rigid living rules that so wrapped up the life of a child today. His eyes blinked and took on the loose, mind-wandering gaze that carried him everywhere at once. I watched in delight as his whole body gave over to soaking up moments of awareness with stones, shells, and water-hardened sand ridges. He was joined by the forms of life that call and scurry in harmony with a beach. He sat and walked or squatted, idly probing with fingers and toes. Contentment covered him with a protective shield.

Rasping, breaking the air like a rusty knife, came his mother's irritating voice commanding him to go into the water and not to play along the beach. That's what they came for. That's what they had sacrificed money, time, and duties for. Startled, he tried to obey, but each time the hold of imaginative minutiae halted his mind and eyes and he'd slip into the world of peace.

Again and again came the rusty knife. Finally, in disgust, the mother gathered up their belongings and hauling him by one wrist, she hurried him off to the too hot, too metallic car. Under her breath she muttered about his ungratefulness and foolish response to opportunity. He followed obediently, and they drove off.

And a strange grief welled in my throat. I had seen the death of peace—the gift of peace—rejected. And I prayed for the boy, and I wept for the boy, and I heard God murmur, "I know, I know."

Almost all people have this gift of peace within their grasp—this sense of well-being hiding inside hoping to break out to bring a feeling of joy to their lives. This peace, this sense of wonderment and atonement, evades most people because they do not know how to play. Even when they take time from work to enjoy leisure time activities, they use the same characteristics they do when working. The authors of *Type A Behavior and Your Heart* wrote, "These persons, who can't relax without feeling guilty, tend to over-schedule and over-plan leisure and social activities to the point where even their social life becomes burdensome."[2]

Where Is the Fun?

A business executive described a typical weekend family outing of fun.

"I need two days at the office to recuperate from my weekend play. I pamper that *bleep* boat all weekend, getting it ready for our Sunday afternoon relaxing time on the lake. Then I take the kids out for the ride and I'm in a panic as soon as we leave the boat dock. By the time we're out in the boat fifteen minutes one of the girls says, 'I've got to go potty.' All day long it's one crisis after another, with me finally turning into a hostile monster. I end up screaming 'Don't stand up,' 'Sit down,' 'Don't lean over the edge.' The emergencies at the office are child's play compared to my weekend play time."

This man's rasping, rusty knife of rules and fear and frustration cuts the potential peace out of the family fun time.

These scenes on the beach and on the boat are videos of some people's vacation. An irritating, impatient parent in us harshly imprisons us to a life of labor and rules. These demand that even in play we must be serious—that we must not only go to the beach, we must check the water temperatures, analyze the rays of the sun, plan each activity, and leave at exactly two P.M.

We must have something *to do,* never just be.

We must be *active* on schedule, never passive.

We must *make* it happen, never let it happen.

We must *do,* never rest receptively and be renewed.

The parent in us says loudly and constantly, *Don't waste! Be responsible. You came to the beach to swim, now swim. Don't be distracted by the sandpipers strutting, sea oats swaying in the breeze, and people playing and laughing.*

The child in us beckons us to experience the precious something that can be in touch with our sensitive self and with God. The child in us pleads—"Stop! Look! Listen! Take time to love and laugh." The child in us urges us:

- To walk, not run, through life.
- To notice seashells, watch waves, sink our toes in the warm sand, build a sand castle, and then watch the waves slowly wash its walls away.
- To listen to seagulls squeak and to try to catch a platoon of sandpipers sprinting in unison.
- To be amazed by the orange sunset dancing on the crest of white-capped waves.

If by some miracle we let the child in us lure us to such serene moments, the parent's raspy voice says, "You should be ashamed of yourself for wasting that time. What did you do today that's worth doing? How can you take time away from real life to act like a child?"

We fall into this trap of an exaggerated sense of responsibility always to be doing something "worthwhile." Even Jesus' words come under the critical scrutiny of the scholar instead of the saint in us.

"Unless you become as little children you shall not enter the kingdom of heaven" turns into an academic issue to be argued instead of a mystery to be enjoyed. We confuse childishness with childlikeness. As Conrad Hyers wrote, "Many adults quite successfully kill their former childishness but in the process kill also the possibility of a mature childlikeness. Much of what passes for adulthood is, therefore, not maturity but an advanced and hardened stage of adolescence."[3] Adolescence is such a sensitive time of life when what others think of us is so important. Thus we think we must not appear childish; we must take ourselves seriously at all times.

Inability to Play

When questioned about their play time and activities, people said such things as:

"Play! Who has time to play?"

"I can't play. I don't know how."

"Play is something people do when they don't have anything else to do."

"Play is a waste of time."

"Play is for children, and I can't wait for my ten-year-old daughter to get home from school so *I* can play in the snow with her. It just doesn't look right for a thirty-five-year-old woman to be riding a sleigh alone."

The inability to play and thereby be renewed has become a serious problem for many people. For these people, play is not fun and relaxing; it is not intellectually, emotionally, and spiritually renewing. For them, life is a tedious, exhausting, joyless journey most of the time, for their "play" produces as much stress as their jobs.

The problem has become so severe that careers have been carved out of developing methods for helping people cope with this phenomenon. Methods range from "a Mantra a day will keep the stress away" to sophisticated biofeedback systems. While these methods offer help for some, many people continue to search for magical seminars and solutions to their feeling that life ought to be more rewarding. The latter are correct in their search because the problem is more basic to life than most think. Quick, easy methods will not save them.

What Is Play?

Our culture has conditioned many of us to believe that play is: 1) a diversionary activity that prepares us for the important business of living and, 2) not a worthy activity, and one ought to feel guilty for not doing something worthwhile. With these thoughts the only value in play is to serve other causes. The authors of this book not only disagree with these beliefs, they know that in the midst of life's most stressful times there is a joy that can be found through play, worship, and creativity.

Play is a worthy activity with its value established in the order of creation. God creates us with a need to play and when we do not play we suppress a part of our essential nature and suffer the consequences.

Play is an essential ingredient in a family; it enables people to live through and grow from harassing, hurtful, and hostile experiences. Church people who cannot play together cannot grow beyond their differences. Without this magical quality, congregations and synagogues diminish to spiritual battlefields with people fighting over everything from the order of worship to who decorates the fellowship hall. Being unable to play is a sign of an absence of a joyous spirit that unites people.

The characteristics required to play are those needed to worship. Ancient religions designed their play into their worship and celebrated a common spirit through playful and awesome worship. Play and worship combine to renew people intellectually, emotionally, and spiritually. Because these characteristics are fundamental to the human spirit, a few get-well-quick methods will not suddenly release people from compulsions, frustrations, fears, guilt-feelings, and anxiety. To release that spirit of play buried under a mountain of destructive thoughts and hurtful feelings we must search our minds, emotions, and spirits. We must find that special quality of being which God created in us so that we may enjoy ourselves, others, and activities while celebrating life.

The authors hope to help you learn how to *play for your life*—to discover ways to renew yourself emotionally, spiritually, and intellectually.

This book will:

1. Examine the problems with and opportunities in the use of leisure time and play.
2. Explore the relationships between play, work, and religious experiences.

You will be challenged to live the rhythm of life, to throw away the rule-wielding rusty knife that kills peace, and to discover ways to keep life interesting and enjoyable.

Play—A Question

In the search for insights into and solutions to the problems of personal renewal through play, the authors read books and articles, interviewed about 200 people and had over 1200 people fill out the following questionnaire. Before reading others' responses to the questionnaire, write your own responses and then compare them to others.

Play and Worship Assessment

Male _____ Female _____

1. Do you take time to play? If so, how much time?
   per day _____ per week _____
2. When playing, what kind of activities do you enjoy?
3. Do you work at playing? (feels like work)
4. When playing do you think of work (undone deeds, future tasks) much of the time? Or are you "lost" in the activity?

5. When playing, do you feel guilty before, during, after or never?
6. Do you have daily devotionals or some form of meditation? If so, please describe.
7. Do you feel renewed spiritually and emotionally after formal worship?
8. Is worship more like work than play?

When asked to fill out the form, scores of people rebelled, demanding a definition of play. Intentionally we did not define the word play for many reasons. The Oxford Universal Dictionary gives fifty-three definitions for play. Think of the many ways the word play is used:

Play fair	Play with words
Play for time	Free play of the mind
Play on feelings	Make a play for
Play out	Play house
Play possum	Play tricks
Play up to	Play a hunch
Playboy	Play at—pretend
Playgirl	Play into someone's hands
Play act	Play one's cards right
Playmate	Playground
Play with ideas	Play room
Play it straight	Play therapy
"Play"—drama	Play loose and fast
Play one's part	Play the horses
Play around	He played his mother against his wife
Play—contest	Others
Play—cut up	

A Word with Many Meanings

These are but a few of the ways the word is used. It is a word that has so many meanings it is difficult to know exactly what people mean when they use it. So instead of defining play, the authors will *describe* what they and others consider play.

What one person considers play another thinks of as work.

While a plumber worked on the sink, Loren talked with him and watched every turn of the wrench so that this hi-tech entrepreneur would not be needed the next time the sink stopped up.

"How long have you been a plumber?" asked Loren.

"Three years. It took me five years to learn enough from books to pass the state test."

Noticing that the man was about forty years old, Loren asked what he did before that.

"I was in prison for ten years. I killed a man. He deserved it," the plumber said with the same emotion one would use when ordering a Big Mac. "Prison is not so bad . . . but there are some crazy people in there."

Loren's interest peaked as he anticipated tales of bizarre behavior and colorful characters.

"Tell me about it."

"The craziest man I met," the plumber said, "was a man who read books. Can you imagine that? He sat in his cell and read books and didn't have to."

Loren went downstairs and closed the door to his study.

Most reading is play for Loren and a terrible punishment for this particular plumber. (This is in no way a reflection on plumbers. Another plumber we know enjoys reading.)

A Perspective on Play

What is play for some people is work for others. For some people working on the house on weekends is play. For others it is condemnation to boredom.

Sitting under a shade tree on a warm summer day with the cool breeze gently blowing is the ultimate gift of personal renewal for some. After five minutes another person starts pruning the tree.

Coach George can turn a little league baseball game into a World War II-type activity and get an ulcer in one season while "playing." Coach Jim approaches the game playfully and enjoys all the young players regardless of their skills and competitive spirit.

Attending the opera is play for some people; for others it is a boring, mysterious night of listening to people in peculiar costumes scream at each other in a foreign language.

Listening to and watching a Prince rock concert is the ultimate play activity for some; for others, it is an excruciating and deafening night of listening to one person in a weird outfit yell at thousands.

Fishing is fun for some and drudgery for others. Many, many years ago when Loren was courting Catherine, he took her fishing on a date. He fished. Catherine became pensive. When Loren asked Catherine what was troubling her, she said, "I didn't think we were *really* going to fish." After the appropriate apology was made, Catherine explained that she and her father went "fishing" almost every weekend when she was a child, but never actually fished. They played in the beach sand, built sand castles, ran, talked, and just enjoyed each other. Loren put his fishing tackle in the car.

Looking at Leisure

What is play? Play *may* be what we do with our leisure periods, which has been described as discretionary time. Leisure time is that part of a day or week or year when our actions are not structured by work, family obligations, and personal duties. After we work eight to twelve hours on the job, drive children to and from soccer practice, take them to the dentist, pay the bills, buy groceries, cook food, wash dishes, eat the obligatory three meals and two snacks, and sleep six to eight hours, leisure time is what is left over. At least, that is what many people consider leisure time in which they may play. It is leftover time *after* the main business of living is over. They do not consider play an essential ingredient in a balanced life, only a luxury to be enjoyed *if* there is time—and there seldom is.

In addition to the problem of having too much to do,

there is the problem created by a self-defeating idea about work and play. Ideas about work and play are often instilled by parents.

When asked what his parents told him about work and play, Chris replied hostilely, "My father was impossible. He told me almost daily, 'We play after the work is done.'" Chris added, "Farm work is never done. Therefore, my father thought it was a disgrace when I even talked about playing. And when I sneaked off to play in the hayloft and he caught me, he punished me. I grew up thinking that play was one of the seven deadly sins."

This problem is compounded when we realize that in most vocations the job is never done. We cannot complete the job and say it is finished. There is always more to be done, because the profession is a continuous process.

The business executive is always in the process of changing to keep pace with the technology and competition. Today's computer is tomorrow's antique. The homemaker finishes cooking one meal, or cleaning one room, or transporting one child, only to see six other things that need doing. Clergy live daily with "the distribution of the neglects." That is, there are always more things that need doing than one can do. In the church and in many other organizations, committees have a way of reproducing—one meeting leads to three meetings.

The Need for Renewal

If we wait until we have discretionary time to play, most of us will not play. The results of such action and attitudes are usually disastrous. For if we do not take time to renew ourselves emotionally and spiritually, our work will suffer, our children and spouse and friends will irritate us—and we them. Food will go untasted as we mindlessly shovel it into our mouths, and we will awaken from a night's sleep tired.

This attitude and action often leads to what has been popularly called burnout. Examine the following phases of burnout to see if you have been tempting fate.

The Phases of Burnout

One cause of burnout is taking ourselves too seriously all the time. In the first of the three stages of burnout, we begin to take ourselves, our problems, and our power (the ability to influence others to do what we want them to do) very seriously. We may exaggerate our sense of responsibility and influence over others. The firm, the organization, and the family will fail unless we make all the right decisions—and work eighteen hours a day! Yet, there is the haunting suspicion that maybe life will progress smoothly even if we do not get our way. With these confusing feelings of frustration and anxiety (fear of the future) making us uncomfortable, we begin to feel as though we are losing control of people and events. It seems that our actions, decisions, and ideas are not making much difference. People and events appear unaffected by what we say and want and expect.

Workaholic tendencies may set in. We try harder and work longer and it seems get less results. Yet, we keep busy, doing something all the time. This work/work syndrome reminds one of the phrase, "Efficient people get things done right. Effective people get the right things done." The temptation is to become efficient, fiddling with details. Some people go so far as to straighten out their desk, write unnecessary memos, and clean the house. They retreat to tasks they can control and ignore those that threaten to defeat them. This behavior is accompanied by thoughts such as "It's easier to do than delegate" and "I'm the only one who can do the job right."

Exhaustion and fatigue set in. Frustration mounts. (Incidentally, according to a recent article, fatigue is the seventh most frequent reason people give for visiting a physician.)

Because the predominant feeling affecting us in stage I of burnout is frustration and because many people have difficulty playing "playfully" when frustrated, we need to stop the problem before it reaches stage II.

3

A Constructive Use of Frustration

People get frustrated when they do not get their own way. The baby will not stop crying in the restaurant, the spouse is too busy to listen, the manager will not state specifically what is expected. Frustration is a signal that things are not as we want them.

Frustration is the *feeling* caused when a goal is not attained or not attainable at the desired time. The report is due at noon. The phone rings repeatedly with someone needing information or expecting us to do something for them. By 11:30 A.M. we are not only frustrated, we resent every person who interrupts us.

Frustration affects the whole person and has a far-reaching effect on a person's personality and production. When they are frustrated, people feel handcuffed, trapped, paralyzed, indecisive, tense, and powerless. They are caught with energy battling to be released and someone—or something—blocking the exits to satisfaction.

People react differently to frustration. There are the

aggressive actions of cursing, hitting people or objects, driving dangerously, making sarcastic remarks, and other acts limited only by imagination and experience.

Passive reactions to frustration include eating, sleeping, crying, procrastinating, pouting, working when one should be playing—and playing when one should be working. People who cannot control family relationships often work long hours, not only to avoid the feeling of powerlessness at home but to remain in the arena of life where they feel powerful, manipulating people, problems, and projects. People frustrated at work often escape to the golf course, tennis courts, jogging trail, and home where they feel partially in control.

Some Facts about Frustration

Frustration evokes aggressive feelings of anger, resentment, and hostility. It also calls forth passive feelings of failure, worthlessness, impotency, and self-pity.

We can anticipate being frustrated much of the time when:

1. We expect everything and everyone to be and do what we want them to—*all the time.* If we need to control everything and everyone, we will be frustrated much of the time.
2. We wait until the last minute to complete tasks. Procrastination puts pressure on us to produce our best instantly; frustration builds as deadlines near.
3. We do not give the mind time to yield its best results through the creative process. Knowing that with more time one could do much better is not only frustrating, it often affects one's self-esteem.

Though frustration can pronounce the death knell on creative thinking and maximum efficiency and a playful spirit, it need not be so. Frustration can be channeled for creative, constructive work, living, and playing, thereby enhancing feelings of confidence and self-worth. Though it can make us uncomfortable, frustration can signal the fact that an exciting challenge is ahead—or it may be interpreted as an ominous sign that failure is in the future. Often, the difference between the two responses is not in the facts of the situation; it is in how one chooses to perceive the problem. One person perceives an active child as an irritating interruption while another person sees an interesting, energetic young person with whom to play. One person perceives the organization as conservative, rigid, and handicapped with rules and red tape. Another person sees the challenge of changing the organization. The first person is frustrated, irritated, resentful, and tired much of the time. The second person is interested, excited, and energetic most of the time. The first person blames others for those uncomfortable feelings; a second person accepts responsibility for doing something about the situation and any frustration experienced.

To use frustration creatively, one must become intellectually aware of it as a problem deserving special attention. Most people ignore this fact. They become so occupied with the goal desired they do not *think* about the frustration itself. Obsessively they gaze at the problem or the people between them and the goal, and their feelings cloud their vision and thinking. Frustration not only compounds a problem, it *is* a problem. It merits one's best thinking and acting.

Eight Steps to Creative Use of Frustration

1. Identify the specific people, goals, tasks, and expectations one thinks are causing the frustration. Make a list of everything related to the frustration. A simple procedure is to relax in a chair, close one's eyes, and with pen in hand, record the items as they flash across the mental screen.
2. Divide the list into two categories—those items we can do something about and those that are beyond our control. We can write the report, make a

telephone call, and confront the manager or spouse to work on a problem; we may not be able to cure a disease, make a mechanic work on our car today, or our spouse attend the ballet.

3. Make a list of the controllable items we will do and scratch the others from the "ought to" list. We may decide to confront the manager with our limitation of time and seek a solution to the dilemma of too much to do and too little time in which to do it. Instead of living with too many missed deadlines, the manager may decide to call a conference to analyze the problems and to design specific ways to solve them. We choose to do something, which gives us a feeling of being in control of some part of life.
4. With those items we cannot control, we consciously work on our attitude. Though we do not have the power to get what we want in these situations, we *can* choose our attitude. We can be angry and become resentful and let the feelings contaminate all of life and handicap our creative, productive efforts and relationships. Or, we can accept our powerlessness in the situation and choose to use our emotional energies on more satisfying projects, which is an affirmation of self-autonomy.
5. We must decide *how* we are going to do what, listing specific actions needed to accomplish each task.
6. Place the tasks in the order of their importance. Decide which ones need immediate attention and which tasks can be accomplished later. A family problem may be more important than an office irritation, thereby requiring our creative energies first—or an office problem may demand our immediate attention while a family irritation lingers one more day.
7. Decide *when* to do each task. Each task is given an appointment on our calendar. Usually when an "ought to" has been given a "date," it will move to the recesses of the mind and wait its turn.

8. *Now,* instead of gazing at and admiring our clever organization, we take the first action to accomplish a small part of one task. We are in control of some part of our life and are *doing* something about what we feel and want. The signal of frustration has been used to motivate us to take charge of and responsibility for our working and playing, our thinking and feeling, and our living and loving.

Play—Rapture and Peak Experience?

If the trend toward burnout is not reversed at the frustration stage, we enter phase II, which is characterized by resentment. We resent people, especially those who seem to have some control over us. Our boss, spouse, parent, and children may become objects of our criticism. Nit-picking the behavior of others, noticing only what they do wrong and seldom seeing the good, we lose sight of the basic purposes of our jobs, family relations, and friendships. We lose sight of the reasons for bothering with all the duties and details of life and focus on less important matters. The typographical error, dinner menu, dripping faucet, and driving a son to ball practice unduly upset us. The little things become the big issues in life.

Gradually we withdraw from others and become cold, uncaring, and unsympathetic. Though we do not admit it to ourselves, and may not even recognize it, we try to turn all concerns into objective problems to be solved, instead of considering the people who are affected by the problems. Somehow we suppress our warmer feelings of affection, empathy, and love to protect ourselves emotionally. We find excuses to stay away from most people. Reading, working or fussing with projects, we spend less time with people in the office, at home or socially. Fantasies of revenge or heroic deeds may slip into our minds.

As we feel more and more powerless, resentment ferments and relationships usually deteriorate further. Taking oneself too seriously reaches a painfully new high in this phase of burnout.

Questions We Must Face

Answering the following questions may help you identify the problems before they cause any more difficulties and pain:

1. Do you think and feel you have been treated unjustly? Were you passed up for a promotion, ignored when praise was due, criticized severely by someone, or neglected by family or friends? Often when people experience burnout they become supersensitive to other's actions toward and words about them. What, in better days, would be forgiven or even not noticed may strike a stinging blow to one's weakened ego.
2. Are your actions and attitudes causing people to avoid you? Have you laughed less and complained more recently? Do you exude hostility and sadness, or are you interesting and fun to be with?
3. Have you talked honestly to a friend about your problems? Most people find talking to a friend relieves some of the inner pressure and puts the problems in proper perspective. During our research on play, scores of people took time to thank us for raising the issue of work and play. By reflecting on their lives, they discovered they had been neglecting some of their most important values. Simple

things, like expressing appreciation to a spouse or friend, or taking time to laugh and to play with one's children, had been forgotten.

4. Have you taken the time to play alone or with people? Play is a way of stepping out of our problems for awhile. One reason play renews us emotionally and spiritually is that when playing, we lose a sense of time: the loss of time consciousness is an essential element in play that renews. When "lost" in play, people are not conscious of or plagued by the clock. Though all of life may seem to be counted by minutes and ruled by calendars and to-do lists, when people play, these rules are suspended. One may play for an hour or four hours and not be conscious of how much time has expired.

The ability to become intellectually and emotionally absorbed in an activity is a natural characteristic of people and either is encouraged or discouraged when one is a child. One of the unreasonable expectations parents have of children is for them to know exactly how long one hour is. "Be home at 5:45 for dinner," father tells ten-year-old Junior. When Junior is fifteen minutes late, father scolds and may punish his son for being late, for not being responsible. While throwing the ball, or playing soccer in the park, or watching butterflies flirt with flowers, Junior gets lost in the activity. Time ceases to exist. The world is too interesting to think about dinner or parents or 5:45 P.M. If Junior's parents are successful in their training, Junior will learn never to let himself get lost in fun activities. He will become so time-conscious and so "responsible" he will lose the capacity to play, and that will affect his coping capacities when, as an adult, life becomes too responsible and stressful in stage III of burnout. The challenge for parents is to teach their children to be responsible without killing their capacity to play spontaneously in and with the everyday wonders of life.

Blaming and Burnout

In stage III of burnout, we become disgusted with almost everyone and everything. Apathy overcomes us and we simply cease caring. Life becomes an almost robot-type existence flavored with our cynicism. Blaming others for our problems is a daily ritual.

"If my manager was not so bossy, I would work harder."

"If Fred would lose weight, I'd be more loving."

"It's the secretary's job to keep my calendar correct. She knows she should remind me to buy George an anniversary present."

"Ms. Smith is always happy. It's disgusting and distracting. How can people get any work done with all that fun and laughter going on?"

We become bitter and project our problems on to others with "it's their fault that I don't . . . ." And "if only they would . . . , then I would . . . ."

Even the act of sex between a husband and wife becomes a duty rather than a celebration of mutual love.

Finally, we resign ourselves to a boring, cynical existence, working for a paycheck instead of looking forward to the challenge of the job. Retirement becomes a daily fantasy and the intervening years are looked upon as a prison sentence imposed by fate. The children become irritations to be endured instead of mixed blessings with whom to grow and to enjoy life. Even our play becomes an obligation. In funereal tones we say, "It's our anniversary. Let's go to the theatre." Or "I guess we will have to take another vacation this year."

By this point in the burnout process we have become the center of the universe, the subject of all life; we are the fallen god of our destiny. Our disappointment in and distrust of ourselves, other people, and God drives us to think about ourselves and our problems twenty-four hours a day. That leads to serious emotional, spiritual, intellectual, and physical paralysis.

At such times, we need regular relief from thinking about and taking ourselves so seriously. We need to recapture the capacity to play—to call forth that playful spirit in us, which is buried beneath a crust of "have tos," "ought tos," and "musts" and "must nots." This is not to deny the complexity of such a state of mind and emotions, but to affirm the need to drive deep within ourselves to retrieve a God-given capacity that has been misplaced in our minds and suppressed in our emotions.

Losing Ourselves in Play

Play helps us regain perspective on life, for while playing we forget ourselves. We are "lost" in the activity. We do not think about what we are doing, we just do it. We do not analyze or ponder feelings, we just enjoy feelings. When we play, past and present problems are not determining our feelings, or affecting our action, or contaminating our thinking. We are free inside to be totally present with whomever or whatever is there to enjoy. There aren't any guilt feelings or jealousies or hatreds or failures to spoil our joy. The future, with all its fears, anxieties, goals and fantasies, is forced to the mental file cabinet marked "to be considered later."

In *Sermons in a Monastery,* the monk and sometimes hermit, Matthew Kelty, captured the thought when he wrote:

"Reality can be perceived in its fullness only when it is perceived in rapture. Rapture is a quality of the pure in heart. To perceive reality in its fullness, therefore, we must be pure of heart. But rapture is also a quality of play. We may suspect, then, that in play lies a road to purity of heart . . . that in play we are schooled in purity of heart, experience rapture and perceive the fullness of reality."[1]

Rapture and Play

Is Kelty talking about our play? *Rapture.* What a strange word to use when talking about play. Could he be referring to the same reality Jesus tried to reveal when he said, "Unless you become as little children you shall not see the kingdom of heaven"?

Is Kelty's rapture the same reality Abraham Maslow referred to as "peak experience"? In writing about how peak experiences through music, art, mathematics, and so on may be used in education, Maslow concluded, "We may be able to use those experiences that most easily produce ecstasy, that most easily produce revelations, experiences, illuminations, bliss, and rapture experiences."[2]

Is Kelty's rapture similar to the magical moment of creativity when *the* answer, the insight, the long sought-after solution breaks into the open with a "Eureka!—I found it." This moment is always followed by feelings of ecstasy.

Can you identify with Kelty's rapture? Try it. Remember a time, a place, a person, or an event in which you forgot yourself for awhile. Then you emerged from the play time feeling fresh emotionally, or spiritually, or intellectually or all of the above. It may have happened while playing with a child (or playing with your parents as a child), or coping with a problem, or watching a sunset, or fishing, or talking with a friend, or during a celebrative worship. In such moments we lose touch with time and tasks and get in touch with a reality that is part of us—a holy part of us.

If we have not had a renewing experience lately, we are denying, repressing, suppressing, or blocking in some way that part of ourselves which God created to keep us joyously alive. Considering how much people are preoccupied with burnout, stress, and conflict, we have to conclude with Kelty that, "because our culture does not know how to play, we as a people are not characterized by purity of heart, nevertheless, the instinct to play abides in every person and waits to be developed in order to express itself."[1]

Peak Experiences and Play

What is play and what prevents many people from having peak experiences and experiencing rapture and knowing the renewing feeling of ecstasy?

A friend of ours offers this insight:

"A couple needs to be sensitive to one another's peak experiences. In my first marriage, I would come home from fishing in a mood of rapture and meet a barrage of jealousy demanding equal time. She would sometimes take equal time and go shopping, which would make a fishing trip cost $100 plus.

"It is so pleasant now to be happy about an experience and come home to someone who is excited about my good fortune."

5

Play—Competition

While having lunch with two friends on the River Walk in San Antonio, Texas, instead of totally relaxing, Loren used the otherwise playful time to research play. Before the spicy enchiladas and refried beans arrived, Loren asked, "Can you play? I mean let yourself be playful?"

Wayne said, "Not me. Everything is competition to me."

Jack added, "No. I just can't play. The competitive drive is always present whether I'm jogging, preaching, or conducting a class."

Jack described the following incident. He was coaching a soccer team on which his eight-year-old son played. At half-time, Jack's team was losing. Jack gave a rousing pep talk—"You can win. You can do it. You're better soccer players than they are. Now let's go out there and show them what real soccer is." He could tell he was getting the players "fired up" for the second half. His son, Chad, got caught up in the rhetoric and blurted out enthusiastically the beautiful, affirming words his father had taught him.

"It matters not whether you win or lose. It's how you play the game. Remember! We're all winners whether we win or lose."

"Not now, Chad. Not now," Jack urged.

The competitive spirit drives some people to turn all of life into contests and prevents them from playing in a playful spirit. Competition operates on the premise that there must be a winner and a loser. If the competitive drive motivates us in *everything* we do, whether playing is fun or frustrating is determined by the outcome of the contest. If competitors win, it is fun and seems to give them additional energy. If competitors lose, it is frustrating, saddening, and angering or all three and seems to sap energy. Winners of a contest are usually renewed by the play; losers are sapped of all energy and are often depressed.

Winning and Losing

To capture the "thrill of victory and the agony of defeat," TV cameras zoom in on basketball players immediately following the game. The players in blue uniforms jump up and down and hug each other, slap each other's hands (known as high fives), cut the net from the rim of the basket, and carry the coach about on their shoulders. They are happy, energy exuding from every pore, even though they just finished running, jumping, punching, and shoving for the better part of an hour.

The camera zooms to the team in orange. Some players sit on the bench, or on the court, with their hands over their faces while tears slip between their fingers. Others appear comatose, staring into space. Strolling to the dressing room, they appear to have hardly enough energy to lift their feet, much less respond to the blue players who keep saying to them, "Nice game, nice game," while shaking their hands.

The camera zooms to the stands, focusing on people laughing and hugging each other, holding up their index fingers to signal that their team is best in spite of their ten losses. Other fans look disgustedly at the scoreboard and resentfully at the happy faces. The victorious fans celebrate in a restaurant after the game; the losing fans talk about firing the coach while they recount his coaching mistakes.

Compulsive Competitors

It is never "only a game" for compulsive competitors, whether they are participants in or spectators of the game. It is a way of life that drives people to success and failure. The competitive spirit drives people to success, and that is helpful in getting out of life what we need and much of what we want. But when *everything* is competition, this drive can cause problems.

This relentless taskmaster seldom lets us relax and be renewed because *everything* is competition. Marriage may become an endless contest of who can get the upper hand in the relationship, who is going to decide who manages the money, who is the best cook, who is wisest in disciplining the children (for my children must look better, act better, and make better grades in school than their cousins and classmates). The competitive spirit can turn a marriage into a contest with the alarm clock starting a new decathlon every day.

The compulsive competitor can convert a friendly game of golf, or tennis, or bridge, or Trivial Pursuit into an emotional life-or-death issue. It can make a job an eight- or twelve- or sixteen-hour ordeal of tension.

Tom began his career with the architectural firm with the goal of becoming a partner. His high intelligence, drive to excel, and dedication to the firm impressed the partners in the firm during Tom's first year. He was often consulted on major decisions. Ten years later the president retired, vacating a position on the board. It was obvious to Tom that he would be chosen for a vice-presidency and given a seat on the board. When someone else was chosen, Tom went into depression. He could not understand why he was passed over for the promotion. The reason was obvious to everyone but Tom.

To Compete or Cooperate?

Throughout his career, Tom competed with everyone. He was quick to criticize other's work and character, intolerant of failure (his and others), and perceived every meeting as a contest in which he had to contribute more than anyone else, while demonstrating his superior intelligence. Tom did not know when to compete and when to cooperate. He did not know when to drive his ideas full force ahead to overpower opposition and when to back off and let things happen.

The same characteristics pervaded his home. He did not play with his son, he competed against him. It wasn't enough for Johnny to play little league baseball, Johnny had to lead the league in hitting or be considered a failure. Everything was competition, therefore, Tom seldom if ever had a relaxing, renewing moment in his life. He never learned to play playfully and thus lived with inner tension and a sense of urgency all day every day.

What causes Tom and other compulsive competitors to race through life in high gear all the time? At least one cause is related to the *need* to succeed. For some people success determines self-worth. Their feelings of worth are conditioned by how successful they are. If they succeed, they feel good about themselves; if they fail, they feel worthless. This is probably true of most of us to a certain degree. We feel better when we succeed than when we fail. But with a compulsive competitor, these feelings are not confined to the particular goal or activity in which they are involved. There is more involved than just being disappointed in shooting a bad round of golf or cooking a tasteless dinner or writing an unacceptable report. The thoughts and feelings are more fundamental than "I am a failure as a tennis player or housekeeper or manager."

Compulsive competitors feel like failures as human beings with every defeat and failure. Success and failure are Being problems as they ride an emotional roller coaster of ups and downs. When we have to be successful in everything, everything is competition. There is not any time to play playfully because too much is at stake. In fact, compulsive competitors' bodies, minds, and emotions do not recognize leisure time. They use their leisure time to express the same obsessions they do in their work. They continue to drive their emotional, intellectual, and spiritual motors in high gear. Giving and grabbing scraps of life, they never have time to receive and to accept gifts from other people—and God! They are too busy proving their value to discover and experience their worth by relaxing and receiving the gifts of joy God has created within them. They rush past the experience described by Isaiah, "You shall go out in joy, and be led forth in peace" (55:12).

The author of Ephesians suggested that we cannot earn a sense of self-worth with a symbolic rosary of victories when he wrote, "By grace you have been saved through faith; and this is not your own doing, it is a gift of God—not because of works, lest any man should boast" (Ephesians 2:8–9).

Most high achievers occasionally slip into the compulsive competitor's way of life. (The authors know this from experience.) When we do, we need some way or someone to help us stop, look, and listen to that which is deep within us and others—to try to recapture the rhythm of life God created for us to live. It is not easy.

Some people compete because it is fun to play in a contest. It is fun trying to improve one's skills as a tennis player, golfer, bowler, bridge player, singer, or art critic—competing against oneself as well as others. These friendly competitors are not overly ecstatic when they win nor do they get depressed when they lose. They enjoy the contest, win or lose, because they can accept defeat without feeling that their worth as a person has been diminished.

Measuring "Success"

A question to ask ourselves is how do we determine success? What criteria do we use? We may keep the score of a golf match or a bridge game, yet the success of the event may not be judged by who won or who lost. It may not even be decided by how well we played. For some people the success of the happening is usually not considered except in a casual way. A father putting his arm around his daughter as they walk off the tennis court saying, "I really enjoyed playing with you today," is not thinking about who won and who lost, because in such situations both are winners.

In renewing play there are not external, measurable criteria for success. The "success" of the event or happening is inherent in the play. There is a movement in the United States to play games without keeping score—volleyball, basketball, baseball, and so on. It is probably a good idea for those who are prepared for it. Unfortunately, Catharine and Loren still struggle with the problem and keep score. Yet, they know that the greatest joy and renewal comes when they play playfully without emphasizing the score.

How Wayne "Won"

Wayne related the following when describing his competitive nature.

"Saturday was my day off, so I decided to give Adam, my four-year-old son, an hour of my time and then go to the office. We got on the bicycle at 10:00 A.M. Adam was perched on the seat behind me. After riding around town for about thirty minutes, I had to stop to rest. We pulled in behind some stores, stopped, and after dismounting, Adam and I sat under a shade tree. Adam inspected the surroundings. The Dempsey dumpster was overflowing with cast out vegetables, meats, boxes, and smelly objects of unknown origin. It was a repulsive sight, but I needed the rest.

"After about ten minutes, Adam said, 'This is a beautiful place.' I looked at the cast-off casualties of commerce again to see if I had missed something. No. This was trash—smelly, ugly, repulsive trash.

"Then Adam said, 'I guess this is the best day of my life.'"

After the lump left Wayne's throat, he towed Adam around town for several hours. Wayne was exhausted, felt the consequences of his excessive exercise, but was renewed personally.

One of the most difficult things for some of us to learn is when to compete and when to cooperate, when to push ourselves to accomplish a goal and when to let ourselves simply enjoy the moment.

Worship Our Work

The English historian, Arnold Toynbee, wrote:

> In my attitude about work, I am American-minded. To be always working and still at full stretch has been laid upon me by my conscience or duty. This enslavement to work for work's sake is, I suppose, irrational; but thinking so would not liberate me. If I slacked or even just slackened, I would be conscience-stricken and therefore uneasy and unhappy, so this spur seems likely to continue to drive me on so long as I have any working power left in me.[1]

When filling out the questionnaire, hundreds of people said they felt guilty when they played. Some felt guilty just planning to play. Our culture teaches many of us that work is virtuous and play is frivolous. Work is worthy; play is useless. Harold Schwarz passed the following rebellious couplet to us entitled "Three American Heresies":

> We worship our work.
> We work at our play.
> We play at our worship.

The first two lines express the prevailing attitude of most Americans. The messages have been passed from one generation to the next in popular sayings.

"Don't be lazy." The condemnatory tone in which the words are delivered convinces children that parents, teachers, friends, and God will not like them if they are lazy. Calling someone lazy usually means no more than "you are not doing what I want you to when I want you to do it." The assumption is everybody ought to be always working or studying or doing something worth doing; doing nothing or playing is the sign of weak character. The following quotes from a chapter in *Paradoxes of Play* entitled, "Too Important to Trust to the Children: In Search for Freedom and Order in Children's Play, 1900–1917," give insight into attitudes about play.[2]

"Two of the leading figures of the playground movement, George E. Johnson and Luther Holsey Gulick, declared at the 1909 P.A.A. Congress that in order to 'insure health, morality, and social good,' playgrounds must be controlled and children taught to play."

"The aims of education and the aims of play became more or less identical by the early 1900s. The aims were loyalty, productivity, morality, citizenship, and responsibility."

"It would become increasingly difficult for children to find opportunities in which they might pursue their own autonomous forms of play."

Pinnacle—or Tentacle?

The Little League World Series televised internationally is the pinnacle of organized children's play, and the end of turning children loose to roam through fields kicking rocks, finding a perfect stick, turning an oatmeal box into a football, and climbing trees. There is usually a recreational director present to point out the rocks, to show them how to select sticks, to give them the football, and to demonstrate how to climb a tree. The spontaneity of play is sacrificed for increased skills, disciplined team effort, and responsibility to the team (loyalty). From the beginning of organized play for children, play has been considered a means to an end. Children's play is supposed to produce adults who are disciplined, responsible, productive and moral.

"Idle hands are the devil's workshop" grew out of the belief that people are basically evil and must be scheduled and supervised all the time to prevent them from doing evil things. As one theologian said, "We only have to watch a two- or three-year-old child for awhile to be convinced of original sin." (He confused children's curiosity, boundless energy, and normal need to test their power with sin, because he made the fatal parental mistake of assuming that parents ought to and could control a two- or three-year-old child.) The belief was that people, especially children, must be kept busy, because the devil was waiting in the shadows to use the little urchins in the service of mayhem and evil. So children must be kept busy working, studying and playing under the watchful eye of an adult. The children are taught to work at their play.

Working at Play

Is it any wonder that we work at our play? The comic strip *Cathy* by Cathy Guisewite captured this theme. In the first frame Cathy is dressed in a leotard, her earphones in place with the cassette in one hand, a magazine in the other. Perspiration pops from her face as she exercises. She is saying, "EXERCISE! I MUST EXERCISE! RUN! WORKOUT! DANCE! GET IN SHAPE!"

The next frame shows her with a pot in one hand, groceries in the other hand, while she dashes about the kitchen. She is saying, "COOK! FIBER . . . SPROUTS . . . ORGANIC GOURMET! I MUST PAMPER MY HEALTHY BODY WITH HEALTHY FOOD!!"

The third frame finds her sitting by her boyfriend on a couch. With hands waving, mouth wide open as if to be shouting, she says, "RELATE! COMMUNICATE! OPEN! WE

MUST CREATE A HEALTHY, LOVING, ENVIABLE RELATIONSHIP!!"

In the fourth frame, Cathy enters her office looking exhausted. Her boss asks, "What brings you in so early, Cathy?"

She answers, "My relaxation time has become more stressful than my work time."

Worshiping Our Work

We not only work at our play, we worship our work. In the Middle Ages, the Roman Catholic Church sold indulgences and has been receiving bad press ever since.[3] According to popular press (which oversimplified the meaning of the practice) one could purchase a ticket for oneself or a deceased loved one, which would bump the person one step higher on the ladder to heaven. It pleased God that one was concerned enough to part with money. During this period, a seller of indulgences abused the practice. He would say, "As soon as the coin in the coffer clings a soul from purgatory springs."

Martin Luther became disturbed over the practice because he thought the church was manipulating the people. With the help of Zwingli, Calvin, Erasmus, and a few other "malcontents" the Protestant Reformation emerged. In spite of a theology of grace proclaimed by prominent preachers, the "Protestant Work Ethic" developed, which said that one works one's way into heaven—the only virtuous person was a hard-working person. The dollar indulgence was traded for a sort of sweaty indulgence earned by sore muscles, long hours of labor, and a sweaty brow. We Protestants tossed in a kicker—the tithe. One could not buy one's way into heaven; one had to work *and* tithe one's way in. Wasting time in frivolous activities displeased the "work-God." The Puritan mind flourished on American soil.

People were taught that you did not come into this world for play or pleasure, but for work and worthy deeds, for seriousness and sacrifice.

Charles Kemp wrote, "As a result of Puritan heritage, some people feel guilty if they enjoy themselves. It is as though anything that is pleasant is wrong. Any time spent in activities other than work is considered wasted."[4]

The Protestant Work Ethic was not only religiously perpetuated, it was sociologically reinforced. How could a society succeed without its people thinking that work was the highest virtue? How would things get done if people were not made to feel guilty for not working hard all the time or, at least, doing something that demonstrated discipline, responsibility, and morality?

In 1926, the president of the National Association of Manufacturers, John E. Edgerton, proclaimed the prevailing attitude, "I regard the five-day week as an unworthy ideal . . . more work and better work is a more inspiring and worthier motto than less work and more pay . . . it is better not to trifle or tamper with God's laws."[5]

"Worship our work." With hard work being equated with virtue and laziness equal to worthlessness, people thought and felt that their worth was determined by how *hard* they worked, not how effectively they accomplished tasks. People were and are taught that they must keep busy doing something.

This belief can cause problems as illustrated by the following incident.

With a twinge of envy, Ellen asked Susan, "How was your vacation in beautiful Vero Beach, Florida?"

"It was not so good," replied Susan.

"What do you mean, 'not so good'? What happened to spoil your vacation?"

"Nothing. No! Nothing bad happened."

"What do you mean, 'nothing'? With all that sunshine, fresh seafood, sand, and ocean in February—I don't understand," probed Ellen.

"Nothing happened," said Susan, "that was the problem. After two days, I was miserable. The last five days almost drove me crazy. I looked at the ocean, walked on the beach, ate seafood, and paced the condo. There wasn't anything to do. I can't do nothing. Yes, I was miserable."

The Horns of Our Dilemma

We are reminded of Walter Kerr's words, "In a contrary and perhaps cruel way the twentieth century has relieved us of labor without at the same time relieving us of the conviction that only labor is meaningful."

In his book, *In Praise of Play,* Robert Neale stings us with these words:

> It is apparent that leisure is threatening to modern man. It provokes boredom in the individual who does not know what to do with himself. It elicits shame in the person who must be important by means of busyness. It gives rise to guilt in anyone who seeks justification by good works and it provokes anxiety in the many whose free time exposes them to the alienation and meaninglessness of their lives. So despite the accusation by some critics that we live in a "fun" society, leisure is more of a problem than a thing of promise.[6]

Can we do "nothing"? Does our leisure time create more stress than our work time?

Leisure time can bring fulfillment or frustration. It can provide satisfaction or emptiness. It can free us or remind us of our imprisonment to a narrow life.

7

Play—A Break from Work

Over 2000 years ago Aristotle wrote, "With what kind of activity is man to occupy his leisure?" The question is as current today as it was then. Today it applies to far more people than in Aristotle's day.

Consider the following predictions:

"By the year 2000, American people are likely to have a four-day work week with a week off every two months and thirteen weeks vacation each year. Most people will spend 40 percent of their time on vacation and 20 percent just relaxing."

Another person predicts that by the year 2000, three percent of the population in the United States will produce all the goods and services for the other 97 percent.

Boris Pregel, past president of the New York Academy of Science, has predicted the work week will soon be reduced to twenty hours, and he is probably closer to the facts than others.

The Opinion Research Corporation reports that "We Americans set aside an average of 27.4 hours a week for leisure." The people the authors interviewed did not report that much play time, but they may not have considered many leisure activities as play.

Looking at Leisure

What are people doing with their leisure? One report suggests that a large percentage of the people moonlight with second jobs. The research also suggested that most people who moonlight do not do it for the extra money. They do it because they do not know how to use their leisure time. They don't know how not to work.

Alex is a forty-five-year-old executive. He is a competent engineer and efficient manager, who lives with the pressure of the rapidly changing computer industry. As if the pressure at the office were not enough, Alex farms 100 acres of tobacco and corn in the evenings and on weekends. Alex literally works all the time. Seldom does he simply relax. Alex does not know how not to work. He needs to learn what Catherine's father urged her to learn when she was a child: "Kid, you've got to learn to do nothing," which was not easier for an energetic ten-year-old to learn than for Alex.

Sarah is a student counselor in a secondary school. After eight hours of empathizing with depressed, angry, and hurt teenagers and talking with depressed, confused, hurt, disappointed, and angry parents, she goes home to the duties of a homemaker, mother, and spouse. At home, when she is not studying students' psychological profiles, she is cooking, washing clothes, dusting, or driving children to their destinations. When confronted with her compulsive working, Sarah said, "I can't just do nothing. I must keep busy even if I have to make up work. I don't have permission to enjoy myself."

Sarah explained that something inside her keeps telling her she does not deserve any happiness.

Is Play a Pleasure?

Is it true what one writer wrote cynically? "To reduce everything to a simple truth: work is less boring than pleasure." Evidently it is for many people.

For those who don't know how not to work, increased leisure time presents many problems.

In a cartoon appearing in "The Globe and Mail" (Canada's national newspaper), students are walking out of an ivy-covered building with *Future Studies* carved on the front of it. A student is saying, "I find the idea of preparing the nation to cope with ever-increasing leisure time somehow inconsistent with the politicians' promise to provide jobs for everyone."

Are we facing the problem Jürgen Moltmann describes in *Theology of Play* when he writes:

> Is life, in which labor is losing its meaning, going to be empty? Will man consider himself irrelevant because he is no longer needed as he once was? Or is he finally going to use his automated world of labor to enjoy God's beauty and the value of his own existence? The man who has been raised by the motto that work alone makes life enjoyable is going to be in for a very rough time. A man who values himself in terms of his usefulness to society must consider his life useless when he is no longer needed.[1]

Trying to come to terms with the traditional female roles of "mothers" and "wives," and the excitement of professional possibilities and emerging "new" roles in society, makes this challenge even more complex for women. (For those struggling with these issues, the authors recommend Lillian B. Rubin's book, *Intimate Strangers,* Harper & Row, 1983.)

Moltmann's prediction is dramatized in literature on retirement.

> Those who make no plans for retirement years receive an average of just thirteen social security checks, and seven out of ten of these people die within two years. Patently, we are talking about men predominantly—accustomed or addicted to work all their life, deriving from that work some sense of importance, and then suddenly deprived by retirement of both their work and their sense of self-worth.[2]

Moltmann's prediction is as true for professional women as for men.

It appears that people are working to remedy this problem. Robert K. Johnston wrote that in 1981 "Leisure-time activities have become the nation's leading industry as measured by people's spending. (244 billion dollars, which was 77 billion more than national defense. Of course, that has changed in recent years.)"[3] Many people are working hard at and spending much money to renew themselves physically, emotionally, and spiritually, yet continue to feel as though they are constantly under stress with little relief from the pressures of life.

We are searching everywhere for solutions to an overactive and underdeveloped life. As Norman Cousins wrote in *Human Options,* "Leisure time in the contemporary world is potentially the greatest gift to the individual, yet it is also a problem of ghastly dimensions. 'It' has thrown man out of joint. People have more time on their hands than their knowledge, interests, or aptitudes can accommodate."[4]

The Prominence of Play

One reason people's play does not renew them in a fundamental way is that play is perceived as a diversionary activity. We say such things as "I've got to get away for a few days. This job is about to get to me." And, "The kids are about to finish me off. I don't think I can handle much more. I need to escape for a few hours." The pressure builds to the point that we want and probably need to get away from whatever it is that is causing the tension.

After a hard day of decision-making at the office, Mack walked into his living room at home. Allie handed him their eighteen-month-old daughter, pointed to three-year-old Mack, Jr., and said, "They're yours. I'll be back in a few hours." She dashed out the door, got into the car, and drove off. Allie escaped.

Though usually not as dramatic as the previous incident, many people think of play as escape from work. The purpose of play for them is to prepare them for work. In other words, they play to work better. As the sociologist, Max Webber, said of many people, "One does not work to live; one lives to work." If we believe that, then play is engaged in so one can work better.

Josef Pieper's words would confuse many people. "A break in one's work, whether of an hour, a day or a week, is still part of the world of work. It is a link in the chain of utilitarian functions. The pause is made for the sake of the work and in order to work, and man is not only refreshed *from* work but *for* work. Leisure is an altogether different matter . . . leisure does not exist for the sake of work."[5]

Robert Neale captures the thought when he writes:

"In a culture that praises work, play is commonly perceived as diversion. Whereas the theorists tend to conceive of play as work, the more informal thinking of the average adult conceives of play as diversion from work . . . To play in order to recover from work is work, and to play in order to return to work is work."[6]

Betty's Problem

During a thirteen-week course on Personal Discipline and Personal Renewal, Betty (a nurse) shared her problem. With a sigh of relief that had a tone of hope in it, she explained:

"Over the past few months, I have been increasingly aware of the fact that my work time far exceeded my play time. It became apparent not only in the number of hours I spent on the job, but in my attitude and outlook on life. I found myself becoming more and more cynical, depressed, and worst of all, detached from my emotions. When a nurse quits caring—becomes stoic—she begins to treat patients as objects and that is bad for patients and the nurse. Knowing that there was a definite problem, I began my search for a solution. I started receiving counseling, thinking that the problem was surely some deeply seeded concern from childhood like all good problems are, but knew I was looking in the wrong place."

Betty discovered that her problem was the way she perceived work and play. Once she was caught in the burnout spiral, even her play became work. Fortunately, during the seminar she recaptured her natural capacity to play with abandonment and to exercise her keen sense of humor, much to the delight of the other seminar participants.

Another seminar participant, Joyce, helped Betty identify part of her problem, when she confessed, "I usually feel guilty when I play. Recently, I have discovered I also feel resentful when I don't play." After filling out the questionnaire, scores of people realized and confessed that they did not play enough, especially with their spouse, and that this lack of play time was causing serious family problems as resentment and tension increased.

Play—a Problem?

The lack of play can cause many problems in our family, friendships, and work. Working at play can perpetuate problems of increasing stress and disappointment.

As John Cheever said, "The main emotion of the adult Northwestern American who has had all the advantages of wealth, education, and culture is disappointment.

"Work is disappointing. In spite of all the talk about making work more creative and self-fulfilling, most people hate their jobs, and with good reason. Most work in modern technological societies is intolerably dull and repetitive."[7]

Though we know that some people hate their jobs because the jobs are dull, let us hope that most people do not. But for those who do, play is essential in more ways than for those who enjoy their jobs.

With the increased leisure-time, we need to learn how to see and to experience play as more than a diversionary activity. It can be and is for many people.

Play and Guilt Feelings

Several years ago when Loren was an avid golfer, he was playing more golf than he should have been. There were times when he should have been calling on clients instead of lining up putts. Realizing that this problem was about to get out of hand, he made a rule that was to control the playful behavior. The next time that he discovered he was playing golf when he should be working, he would penalize himself with a six-month ban from the golf course.

A few weeks after establishing the rule, he was playing with his regular foursome. He missed a three-foot putt. "How could I miss that putt?" he mumbled to himself. Then the terrible truth flashed in his mind. He was feeling guilty for not working, and therefore was having trouble concentrating on the golf game.

Shoving his putter in the golf bag while reaching for his wallet, he explained briefly the situation to the other three golfers. Though it was only the third hole, he paid his opponent six dollars (the most he could have lost) and started walking to the clubhouse. The other golfers pleaded, then threatened, and finally shouted uncomplimentary words after Loren. But he left the course anyway.

Because guilt feelings are such saboteurs of satisfaction in playing, we will examine the effects guilt feelings have on people.

I Feel Guilty When I'm Having Fun

When we feel guilty for and when playing, we are not renewed, refreshed, and re-energized. The weight of the guilt feelings on our minds and emotions saps energy instead of giving it. The diversionary activity does not even give us an emotional and "intellectual" break from our work. For when we feel guilty, our mind and emotions work overtime to relieve the tension we feel. Regardless of what we are doing, work or play, the inner alienation—the feeling that we are fighting ourselves—continues to plague us.

The consequences of guilt are many. Popular sayings dramatize the far-reaching effects of this internal tormentor.

"Guilt is the very nerve of sorrow." *Horace Bushnell*.

"Guilt once harbored in the conscious breast, intimidates the brave, degrades the great." *Samuel Johnson*.

"Every guilty person is his own hangman." *Seneca*.

"From the body of one guilty deed a thousand ghostly fears and haunting thoughts proceed." *William Wordsworth*.

"The torture of a bad conscience is the hell of a living soul." *John Calvin*.

"A clear conscience is a continual Christmas." *Ellis Yonge* (Catherine's father).

"A good digestion depends upon a good conscience." *Benjamin Disraeli*.

"Like it says in the midrash: 'A guilty man flees when no one's chasing him!'" *Leo Rosten*.

"The Anglo-Saxon conscience does not prevent the Anglo-Saxon from sinning; it merely prevents him from enjoying his sin." *Salvador de Madariago y Rojo.*

Finally a quote from a person who cannot forgive God for not existing, Woody Allen, who speaks through a character in his book, *Side Effects.* "It seemed the world was divided into good and bad people. The good ones slept better, Cloquet thought, while the bad ones seemed to enjoy the waking hours much more."[1]

Allen's tongue-in-cheek assumption seems to be that good people have a conscience that prevents them from violating their beliefs about behavior, and that the bad ones are free from such consequences during the waking hours; the bad ones have great fun but feel guilty afterward.

The questionnaire the authors used for research indicates that people react differently to guilt feelings. Some feel guilty just thinking about playing, others feel guilty while playing, and still others feel guilty after they play but have great fun "during" their "waking hours."

All Are Guilty

Regardless of when or what causes it, most people feel guilty some time. The psychiatrist, Paul Tournier, wrote:

"There are none righteous; all are guilty, as they know and feel more or less clearly. Guilt is no invention of the Bible or of the church. It is present universally in the human soul. Modern psychology confirms this Christian dogma without any reservations. So it does the church justice. 'Far from cultivating guilt,' writes the psychoanalyst Mm. Choisy, 'the church, like psychoanalysis, brings it to consciousness, and this is a way of dispelling it.'"[2]

We can be conditioned by parents, peers, and religion to feel guilty about anything, as illustrated by Joan. Joan, the thirty-eight-year-old mother of two teenage daughters, was going through an early mid-life crisis. Bored with housecleaning, cooking, chauffeuring, refereeing spats over bathroom time and dress distribution, Joan decided to go back to college and carve out a career that would give her ultimate fulfillment. After a year of stressful studies (though she was enjoying her studies and college life), she was still not happy. She went to see a counselor. In the second counseling session the counselor asked Joan to make a list of everything about which she felt guilty. The next week she brought a list of 116 things she thought she *ought* and *ought not* to do. Following is a partial list to demonstrate how susceptible we are to guilt feelings:

1. Talk to John (spouse)
2. Stay home more
3. Cook
4. Iron June's and John's clothes (I iron Jane's)
5. Work to send the girls to college
6. Not say anything bad about John, June and Jane
7. Not ever judge others
8. Help the sick, hurting, oppressed
9. Not talk about my past
10. Not give up—always keep on trying
11. Like children
12. Not waste money
13. *Not take time to play*
14. Not waste time
15. Not buy as many clothes as I do—guilty
16. Not ever appear to others that I feel I'm better than they are
17. Be perfect
18. Feel that God forgives and accepts me no matter what I do (I don't)
19. Obey rules and regulations
20. Do what those in authority tell me to do
21. Go visit my mother's parents—should love them
22. Not leave the children even though my marriage is terrible
23. Not ever get fat
24. Keep the house clean
25. Not be intimate with anyone I do not care about
26. Forgive myself
27. Not scream when I get mad
28. Not lose my temper
29. Always act like a lady
30. Never ask my father for money
31. Not let others get too close to me
32. Express love to June and Jane

33. Have more friends
34. Not smoke
35. Not drink
36. Not lie
37. Not steal
38. Not gossip
39. Not say things that will hurt others
40. Always be working
41. Always go to church on Sundays
42. Be organized
43. Relax more
44. Love others
45. Not cuss
46. Be friendly
47. Exercise
48. Not harm animals
49. Not feel appearance is so important
50. Not sing

How to Resolve Guilt Feelings

The first step in resolving guilt feelings is to identify the thoughts about behavior which cause us to feel guilty. You may want to make your list. As with Joan, once you write them you can more helpfully deal with them—even laugh at a few of the more ridiculous ones.

We can learn what to feel guilty about, and we can unlearn that about which not to feel guilty.

The second step in dealing with guilt feelings is to identify the source of the teaching—who or what taught us to feel guilty about "always working," "not wasting time," and "not taking time to play."

Note the source of the learning by your list of who (and what) evokes guilt feelings:

Mother	School teacher
Father	Boss
Grandmother	Coach (little league type)
Grandfather	Friend
Brother	Other adult

Sister | Church
Television | Other relative
Other

From Joan's list and our list we discover that we have learned rules and regulations for living. Our parents and others placed in our minds and emotions a way of living that is supposed to bring us satisfaction and happiness. Therefore, when we break the rules of this ideal state, we feel guilty. When we feel guilty our self-esteem shrivels.

Paul Tournier put it in perspective: "All inferiority is experienced as guilt." Therefore when we don't live up to the ideal, we feel guilty. It becomes absurd at times—people feel guilty for not being pretty enough, intelligent enough, skilled enough, and scores of other things over which they have no control.

In *Caring,* William Gaylin wrote insightfully on the subject:

"In discussing self-respect, he [Freud] stated that in each individual is internalized an ideal behavior by which the actual self, or ego, judges his own behavior. This, then, is the birth of a conceptual theory of true guilt, for here the anguish of guilt is in the specific sense of personal failure that occurs when we have dishonored our own internal sense of what we ought to be. It is not fear of the others, not fear of punishment, not fear at all. It is disappointment in self."[3]

We fail enough, and thus feel disappointed in ourselves without having to feel guilty for not feeling guilty, as one person expressed it, or for not being perfect, or for not forgiving ourselves.

We might be able to talk ourselves out of feeling guilty over some acts, but it will take time to come to terms with other actions, thoughts, and expectations. We will explore guilt feelings more in the next chapter, but first meet a man with a difficulty that may be your problem with play.

Mark's Problem

Mark's father taught business administration in high school. This master manipulator of schedules arranged his classes so that he never brought work home with him. After school, he rushed home, changed clothes, and went to play. According to the season—he hunted, fished, and gardened. Mark's father played every day and took Mark with him most of the time.

Mark is a clergyman who works most of the time. He doesn't have much time for play. When questioned Mark said, "I was taught two things. One, that I was intelligent and should excel in life—my mother taught me that. Two, that a person ought to play everyday; that work was the price you pay to play, and that play is more important than work. Those two messages clash inside of me. If I don't excel intelligently and professionally I feel guilty. And if I don't play I feel guilty. I can hear my father urging me, 'You ought to be out fishing instead of sitting in that office.'"

Tempting, isn't it?

Play, Guilt, and God

Over forty years ago, when he was fourteen years old, Loren caught the bus from his suburban home to attend a movie in Jacksonville, Florida. After the movie, he went into a "hole-in-the-wall" type restaurant, ordered a hot dog and a coke. It was delicious. (Of course, at that age everything was delicious.) Walking up to the cashier, he asked how much the bill was. The bill was a nickel more than Loren had. He was embarrassed beyond imagination. Promising the proprietor he would return with the nickel, Loren walked out of the restaurant with head bowed.

He kept putting the dutiful deed off. Yet he never forgot the debt for a moment. His secret really embarrassed him; how could he face the man again? Finally, he mustered the courage to live through the imagined agony of the encounter. He would face the man and pay his debt to society and his conscience.

He walked the three miles to town and with each step he felt better. He had finally decided to right the wrong. Again, he would be an honorable boy, a good guy, a fair and honest person. Rounding the corner of Forsythe and Main Streets he briskly marched to the restaurant. A sign on the door shocked his whole system. GONE OUT OF BUSINESS.

My gosh, Loren thought, *I put him out of business.* (People aren't very logical when they feel guilty.)

What a problem! Loren couldn't square his debt. He could not do anything to redeem himself. He could not correct this injustice. Even dropping the nickel in the tin cup of a blind beggar did not relieve the guilt feelings.

Of Guilt and Failure

Guilt feelings do not easily pass from the psyche. Just because we rationally decide that it is foolish to feel guilty about a certain type of action does not erase it from memory. Some specific acts or rules are so deeply imprinted in the memory, that even when we cease to feel guilty about them, the memory of the act or rule lingers to remind us of our failure and disappointment in ourselves. But guilt feelings create more than disappointment in the self. They leave us feeling we have disappointed someone else. That someone is usually our parents or parental substitutes who taught us a code of conduct—the rules for living. To disappoint—to fail—one's parents or parental substitutes is to risk love. It is to risk losing the approval of the ones who validate our existence—the ones who brought us into the world. For many people the worst crime a person can commit is to hurt one's parents in any way. As Fred Bertrand, Jr., wrote, "One is anxious over his guilt because it means to him that he deserves the disapproval and rejection of the loved one."

So if we play instead of improving ourselves with work, study, and other good deeds, we are not living up to our parents' expectation of us; we are failing to be the perfect child. This idea appears almost foolish and it would be except that until we consciously choose our independent way of handling life, we live with the rules our parents planted in us. In the process of selecting *our* rules and principles we may choose the ones our parents did, but they are authentically ours now.

Sources of Guilt

The issue does not end there, for there are two basic sources of guilt feelings. The first one has to do with the behavior we have been discussing and includes feelings and thoughts. For instance, though we may not actually strike back at a person who hurts us, the desire for revenge may make us feel guilty. Fantasizing a promiscuous act causes others to feel guilty. The feelings derived from these thoughts still involve behavior if only in the imagination.

Another dimension to such feelings is that all guilt feels moral and ethical, regardless of the relative importance of the transgression. Feeling guilty about being depressed or physically ill, for fearing retirement, and for being disorganized and for not being happy (from the list of an executive) seems as condemning as being unethical in business dealings, hating and hurting people, and being unfaithful in marriage. The latter type of activity is usually more disturbing, but the increased tension arises from fear—the fear of being found out and punished. Both kinds of acts do equal damage to one's present feelings of disappointment and unworthiness.

The second source of guilt feelings is ontological; that is, one feels unworthy as a human being but does not know why. One feels inadequate, insecure, and condemned for something, but cannot identify the cause. This guilt feeling arises from early childhood experiences as well as behavior-related problems. Usually early in life these people learned that they were not loved. Parental rejection through emotional and/or physical abuse confused them. Or emotionally stoic parents failed to demonstrate in any way that they loved their children. Because children need their parents' love so much, they cannot blame the parents. So they get the feeling that there is something wrong with them. They eventually believe that they are not lovable, and their unlovableness is their own fault.

The Search for Serenity

This sense of inner alienation sends them on a lifetime search for some form of redemption. They want and need to feel worthy, to have some inner peace, and to rest from the inner struggle that condemns them. This search for peace may create a workaholic, or a single-minded person who focuses narrowly on one area of life at a time, or a person so afraid of rejection that the need for approval shows through every smile of appeasement. It often leads the sufferer to one self-help group after another and to religious cults.

Because this guilt relates to Being and not to behavior, it is basically a religious matter. In *Guilt and Grace*, Paul Tournier describes the problem and opportunity.

"Irritation, obduracy, aggressiveness: This is the law of unconscious and repressed guilt. Conversely, pardon and grace produce joy, relaxation and security, the atmosphere in which guilt can become conscious, mature, be openly acknowledged, and in its turn lead onto pardon and grace. So the energy, guilt, becomes a friend, because it leads to the experience of grace."[1]

Needed: A Religious Resolution

The second type of guilt will not let us rest until we resolve it religiously, for it is a Being problem. Jesus spoke to the problem when he said, "Come to me, all who labor and are heavy laden, and I will give you rest" (Matthew 11:28). Jesus was not talking about work; he was referring to the internal strife that we experience when we feel guilty, unworthy, and alienated from God, or what Paul Tillich called alienation from the "Ground of Being."

The problem goes back to the beginning—creation; creation of the world and our creation in it. Examining a few themes from the following scripture makes sense out of this mystery.

> In this the love of God was made manifest among us, that God sent Jesus the Christ into the world, so that we might

> live through him. In this is love, not that we loved God but that he loved us and sent his Son to be the expiation for our sins. Beloved, if God so loved us, we also ought to love one another. No man has ever seen God; if we love one another, God abides in us and God's love is perfected in us (1 John 4:9–12).

John is offering us an understanding of "God is love" that could affect how we think and feel about ourselves, others, and God. We will explore four themes in this scripture without examining *all* the meanings in it.

Themes on Love

The first theme on love is: *God's love is God's nature, not just a nice feeling God occasionally has.* Love is not something God chooses to do; it is who God is. It is in God's nature to love all people—to care about them, what they think, feel, and do. God could not cease to love anymore than a tree could cease being a tree or a bird being a bird. God is love.

The second theme on love is *God's nature, love, was and is revealed through Jesus Christ.* Through Jesus the Christ we may understand that God loves us and, therefore, we are worthy. Just as we did not do anything to cause Being guilt, we did not do anything to cause God to love us. But believing intellectually that God is love does not necessarily resolve the alienation and guilt feelings.

The third theme on love is: *When people experience God's love, they will know God and love others.* The biblical word translated *know* means intimacy. To know God is to be intimate with God. To know God is to feel at home in the universe—to feel as though one belongs to something mysteriously beautiful and good. To know God is more than occasional good feelings during worship service or meditation. As Paul W. Hoon wrote, "The highest knowledge of God is not gained through intellectual endeavor, devotional exercises, or aesthetic contemplation. These may afford knowledge, but they do not provide the ultimate experience." To know God, to be intimate with God, is also to experience intimacy with others. That is, we love and are loved in a relationship that affirms us and the other person.

The fourth theme on love is: *We can love God and others because God loves us and placed the propensity or intense desire to love within us.* The capacity to love is in the order of creation. God creates us for loving and lures us into loving relationships by first loving us. With the affirming experience from another, we may come to the life position that "I am worthy because I am loved," which is to feel "I am worthy of love."[2]

This intimacy is experienced as a gift of grace. Intimacy is God's gift of love through people. In his book *Game Free: A Guide to the Meaning of Intimacy,* Thomas C. Oden records the words people use when describing an intimate relationship.[3] Following are some of them: spontaneity, openness, inner harmony, self-acceptance, closeness, presence, appreciation, sharing, renewing, freedom, awe, surprise, mystery, wholeness, ecstasy, and giftlike quality.

Play—the Touch of the Holy

In an intimate relationship people feel as though they are in touch with something holy, and that they are not judged, condemned, and isolated. They feel a sense of personal worth; they feel forgiven. The guilt feelings created by early life experiences that told us we were not worthy of love give way to a feeling of being "forgiven" in the intimate relationship with God and others. In such experiences we can understand Tournier's words, "Guilt is the driving force towards healing, the decisive power which determines the result of the struggle."[4]

The second level of play touches us at this very point; it speaks to the second level of guilt feelings. For when we play playfully, we are lost in the activity. We forget ourselves. We take a break from our past actions and future goals, and suspend time. During this kind of play we are in touch with that pure love, that childlikeness that trusts and accepts and affirms life, and with the God who created that capacity in us. So people describe this kind of play with such words as: spontaneity, openness, inner harmony, renewing, awe, mystery, wholeness, ecstasy, and self-acceptance.

The second level of play renews us because it is basically a religious experience. One is in touch with God, at the least, in touch with the Godlike quality created in us that affirms our worth.

In *The Christian at Play,* Robert K. Johnston gives hope: "A person engages in play for its own sake, but it can have multiple benefits: 1) A continuing sense of delight or joy, 2) An affirmation of one's united self, 3) The creation of common bonds with one's world, 4) The emancipation of one's spirit so it moves outward toward the sacred, and 5) The relativization of one's workaday world."[5]

Incidentally, have you experienced the second level of play? Does Johnston's "multiple benefits" describe your play? If not, do not despair because there is hope. You have it in you to play for your life and win.

Procrastination and Play

Let us return to that insightful comic strip character, Cathy. She is standing by her boss's desk watching him read a report. Smiling, he says, "I can't believe you wrote this report in one night, Cathy."

Cathy does not speak, but we see her thoughts. *Think how amazed he'd be if he knew I wrote it in the car on the way to work.*

The next frame shows Cathy at her desk with the phone to her ear listening to her boss. "I never thought you'd have those figures done in a week."

Cathy thinks, *Think how amazed he'd be if he knew I did them on my lunch hour.*

The third frame pictures Cathy in her apartment with her mother who evidently just walked in. Her mother says, "How did you manage to clean this place up in one week-end?!"

Cathy thinks, *Think how amazed she'd be if she knew eight bags of garbage went out of here in the last three minutes.*

The last frame shows Cathy alone with arms outstretched saying, "My most stunning accomplishments are destined to go unacknowledged."

Procrastination: Working Better under Pressure?

Cathy illustrates the behavior of habitual procrastinators. She also illustrates the rationale they use when their efforts receive praise. If asked why she waited until the last minute to do her tasks instead of preparing in advance of deadlines, she would most likely respond, "I work better under pressure. In fact, when I try to do work well in advance of deadlines I just can't seem to get going on it."

At least that is what hundreds of habitual procrastinators said when questioned about the phenomenon.

To help you understand how procrastination sabotages your joy in living, a brief review of the characteristics and causes of procrastination will be given. You may want to check the ones that apply to you.

1. *Procrastinators do not have a manageable way of organizing their time and tasks.* Even procrastinators who make To Do Lists, with a firm resolve to follow the lists and time schedules, often become victims of administration by impulse, responding to what happens to them rather than causing things to happen.

2. *Procrastinators have good intentions.* They really believe they are going to do what they agree to do. Ten minutes after saying "yes," they often regret the decision.

3. *Procrastinators usually have a bundle of excuses.*

4. *Procrastinators are charming people* (in public often more than at home). As one sales representative said, "I can't wait to get home so I can quit smiling and start griping. I get so sick of being charming, I could . . . ."

5. *Procrastinators have difficulty saying no.* Smiling, they often agree to do more than they have time to do.

6. *Procrastinators trade a feeling of victory for one of relief.* Instead of celebrating the completion of tough tasks, they give a sigh of relief with "Whee! I'm glad that's over!"

7. *Procrastinators focus on the negative*—on what is not done instead of what is completed. Planning to complete ten tasks today, they check off nine of them and end the day feeling defeated because they did not do the tenth deed.

8. *Procrastinators think they can do better than they show.* They can, but don't.

9. *Procrastinators seldom use evaluation to improve performance.* They are too busy catching up with yesterday's undone deed.

10. *Procrastinators expend much of their time and energy worrying about what they should be doing.* Preoccupation with the past (feeling guilty about half-done jobs) and the future (all those jobs they have to get done today) leaves one numbly suspended between the two.

11. *Procrastinators are seldom emotionally and intellectually totally present at any moment.* When playing, they often feel guilty for not working and when working on one project they are thinking about other "ought tos" they must do. They may even resent not being able to play on such a beautiful day.

12. *Procrastinators feel overwhelmed.*

13. *Procrastinators look for others to rescue them.* This "good fairy" philosophy believes that if I wait long enough someone else will do it or the need for it to be done will vanish.

14. *Procrastinators claim to work better under pressure.*

15. *Procrastinators resent being reminded of their duties,* especially those overdue.

16. *Procrastinators have a low self-image* because they do not live up to their expectations of themselves and fall short of their potential.

17. *Procrastinators often feel powerless and frustrated.*

All people will be able to identify with a few of these characteristics; some will find themselves described by many of them. If you find that you are not enjoying your work and play as much as you should, you just might have a procrastination problem. A person who cannot "live in the moment" shortchanges satisfaction in all of life.

The problem is more complex than many think, for simply knowing how to set priorities, make To Do Lists, and design time lines for projects does not help the habitual procrastinator that much.

Probing Procrastination

To appreciate the complexity of procrastination examine the following causes—how people might become habitual procrastinators.

1. *Parents focused on the negative.*

Sue brings home four "A"s and two "B"s on her report card. Maybe with a courtesy nod to the "A"s, her parents point to the "B"s and say, "Look at those Bs. You can do better than that." No matter what Sue does there is always something more she should have done. "You can do better," echoes in her mind even as an adult—so where her parents left off, she picks up and focuses on the one undone deed, the flaw in the report, and the one criticism, while forgetting the twenty compliments.

2. *Parents rescued.*

After nagging Sue every day for two years to clean up her room, mother or father reasons, "It's easier and takes less time to clean up the room than to get Sue to do it, so I'll clean her room." The "good fairy" is born and Sue learns that if she puts off doing what she dislikes doing long enough, someone else may relieve her of the dirty duty.

3. *Procrastination is one form of personal power.*

It is the way some charming people tell those in authority (spouse, parent, manager), "Nobody tells me what to do," while smiling. They manipulate others by not doing what others expect when they expect it done.

4. *Need for approval.*

A recent survey indicated that the greatest fear for most people in the United States is not fear of death or physical pain, but fear of not being liked.

5. *Fear of rejection* causes many to say "yes" when they should say "no."

6. *Fear of failure.*

7. *Fear of success.*
8. *Lack of skill.*
9. *Lack of information.*
10. *Too much to do.*
11. *Too little to do.* (It causes more procrastination than too much to do.)
12. *Boring tasks.*
13. *Fear of conflict.*
14. *Perfectionism.*

The Procrastinator and the Perfectionist

Inside every procrastinator there is a perfectionist. The research demonstrated that in the same family one child would be a procrastinator and another child would be a perfectionist. The difference in the two is only in how they respond to tasks and people. The perfectionist would say, "I will get this perfect if it drives everyone crazy." It usually does. The procrastinator waits until the last minute, rushes through the job, and when the criticism comes says, "If I had had more time it would've been perfect."

Both usually spend 90 percent of their time on the first 10 percent of the task and have to do the last 90 percent of the task with the remaining 10 percent of the time before the deadline.

Both end the day feeling a sense of incompleteness ("I should have done more and should have done better"), frustration, and anxiousness.

No wonder most people who procrastinate habitually do not enjoy their play or work.

Though the cures for procrastination are more complex than space permits in this writing, a few principles will be listed.

1. *Analyze your procrastination patterns.*
   What type of activities do you procrastinate?
   When do you procrastinate?
   Who is involved when you procrastinate?
2. *Evict the perfectionist.*

Remember: What one person considers perfect, another criticizes. We cannot please everyone. We must decide which tasks deserve our best effort and which ones deserve only adequate attention. All tasks are not equally important. Turn loose of tasks when they are good enough, even though you know that with more time you could improve them.

3. *Clarify your values.*

You have to know and keep in mind what is most important to *you* before you will overcome the tendencies to procrastination (four years of conducting seminars on procrastination proved this).

4. *Set realistic goals.*

Know what you want to do and design a plan for accomplishing the goal.

5. *Learn from experience.*

Examine and evaluate what you do and how you live regularly, and gradually increase your effectiveness and joy in living.

6. *Use time management principles and instruments.*

The market is flooded with this material. Pick and choose the methods most suited for your lifestyle, and include in your scheduling time to play and be renewed or you will continue to sabotage your good intentions.

After reading this, if you still need help with the procrastination problem, use *How to Stop Procrastinating and Start Living* as a workbook.[1] Thousands of people have done so with success (weekly mail to Loren attests to this).

Before leaving this subject, we need to examine briefly one biblical message related to it (there are many).

The Three Meanings of Perfect

In Matthew 5:46–48, Jesus speaks of loving enemies and then concludes, "You, therefore, must be perfect as your heavenly Father is perfect." There are three meanings to the word *perfect:*

First, *perfect* has to do with attitudes and actions toward people. The parallel passage in Luke 6:36 reads, "Be merciful even as God is merciful." To be perfect is to consider the thoughts, feelings, and needs of others in our dealings with them. It does not mean that everything must meet some flawless criteria; it does mean that we are to care about people as God does.

Second, *perfect* is not a static condition. The word implies a process of growth, of change. Perfect suggests a dynamic growing toward increasing sensitivity to others. Though we are not perfect all the time, we can demonstrate perfection (mercy) much of the time. When we show mercy, we are perfect for that act and in that moment.

Third, *perfect* suggests an attitude that relieves us from thinking about ourselves all the time. So long as we try to be perfect, to please others or God, we keep ourselves the center of our attention. In the biblical sense, to be perfect means that God frees us to think and to care about others.

To be perfect is "to get lost"—to forget ourselves—to forget the failures of the past and tomorrow's crowded To Do List so that we can be totally present in a spontaneous, caring way with people whether we are working or playing. That is renewing.

11

Play and Boredom

In Graham Greene's autobiography, *A Sort of Life,* he describes an unusual incident:

> The oppression of boredom soon began to descend. Once on my free day I walked over the hills to Chesterfield and found a dentist. I described to him the symptoms, which I knew well, of an abcess. He tapped a perfectly good tooth with his little mirror and I reacted in the correct way. "Better have it out," he advised.
>
> "Yes," I said, "but with ether."
>
> A few minutes unconsciousness was like a holiday from the world. I had lost a good tooth, but the boredom was for the time dispersed.[1]

This famous English novelist confessed to fighting boredom all his life, including playing Russian roulette several times to jar him out of his lifeless condition. Greene identified with Andre Breton "who wrote in a letter to Cocteau: All my efforts are for the moment directed along one line—conquer boredom. I think of nothing else day or night. Is it an impossible task for someone who gives himself to it wholeheartedly?"

How Prevalent Is the Problem?

Is boredom what causes so many people to go scurrying about the countryside camping, fishing, bird-watching, and swimming? Are many people looking for a few minutes of Greene's "unconsciousness" when they build unneeded additions on their homes, attend movies, concerts, and frequent bars and nightclubs? How prevalent is the problem of boredom?

Are you bored in your job, marriage, and social life?

Consider again John Cheever's words, "Work is disappointing. In spite of all the talk about making work more creative and self-fulfilling, most people hate their jobs, and with good reason. Most work in modern technological societies is intolerably dull and repetitive."

Other writers echo this theme. S. A. Franzmeier asked, "Are you bored? Frustrated by the monotony of your work or leisure activities?" He continues, "Surprisingly, many people today are, even busy executives."

"Boredom is an epidemic. It's the common cold of the psyche," says Sam Keen. The famed psychiatrist, Erich Fromm, called boredom "The illness of the age in which we live."

"Work Is Less Boring Than Pleasure"?

There is a cynical tone to Baudelaire's words in *Journal in Time,* "One must work, if not from taste then at least from despair. For, to reduce everything to a single truth: work is less boring than pleasure."

If these writers are correct in their assessment of the situation and we have to admit that they do speak for many people, then our society is in serious trouble. Consider the following description of boredom from the *Encyclopedia of Psychology.*

> *Boredom.* A psychological condition associated with environmental monotony and characterized by negative effect, loss of interest, wandering attention, low arousal and impaired working efficiency. In its extreme form boredom may give rise to symptoms ranging from depression to agitation and hallucinations, and is being held increasingly responsible for many social problems including delinquency, suicide and marital unhappiness.[2]

Sandra excelled in her work as a social worker and was appropriately recognized in her vocation. She was married to a predictably sensitive, successful lawyer, and "managed" three teenage children. She had social prestige, was a leader in her church, and had every material advantage one would want. Sandra was also a sensitive, caring person.

When asked why she was divorcing her husband she replied, "Boredom. Everything is so predictable. Larry is a fine person. A good husband and father. *But,* I can tell you everything that he and I are going to do for the next year and probably for the next thirty years. I know how and when we're going to have sex, the special celebrations marking anniversaries, birthdays, and every other event that is *supposed* to be celebrated. I know what we're going to argue about and how we're going to make up. The predictability, the boredom, is driving me crazy."

Sandra's life is documented daily in counselors' and lawyers' offices all over the country as thousands of people tell their stories of boredom.

In his usual satirical way Woody Allen describes the dilemma many people feel:

> More than any other time in history, mankind faces a crossroads. One path leads to despair and utter hopelessness. The other to total distinction. Let us pray we have the wisdom to choose correctly. I speak, by the way, not with any sense of futility, but with a panicky conviction of the absolute meaninglessness of existence which could easily be misinterpreted as pessimism.[3]

The companion of boredom is often pessimism. For pessimism produces negative attitude, loss of interest, wandering attention, low arousal, and impaired working efficiency which often leads to depression, agitation, and violence.

Why Are We Bored?

There are many causes of boredom. As we view a few of them, examine your life—your job, marriage, family life, and leisure activities—to identify your boredom rating.

Let us examine boredom on the job.

There are some boring jobs, which have a person doing routine tasks eight hours a day. The misconception many people have is that only routine jobs are boring. Many people become bored with their high stimulation, minute by minute decision-making jobs. Though they are busy and have variety in their work they may become bored because they know they can handle whatever happens. The same type crises occur over and over again and thus the process for handling situations becomes almost routine. Sam Keen observed that "Constant stimulation without interest or fascination increases rather than alleviates fatigue and boredom."

Assembly line laborers, social workers, business executives, and all professional people are candidates for boredom. The cause of boredom, in this case, is the predictability of the job—the lack of challenge.

The best seller book list always has one or two management books on it that advise managers on how to motivate employees. All of them are giving much the same advice. *The One Minute Manager*[4] describes a process:

1. One minute goal setting. Always be sure employees have goals and the criteria for success is clear.
2. One minute reprimand. When mistakes are made confront the employee immediately and affirm the person.
3. One minute praise. Give deserved praise regularly.

As the person learns the job, let the person be responsible for it.

The theme is that people are the most important resource in any organization. When people feel good about themselves they produce good results.

A Feeling of Importance

Whether we are reading *Megatrends, In Search of Excellence,* or one of Peter Drucker's books on management, we hear the same message. For people to maintain interest in their jobs they must feel as though they are important to the process.

If management, from the top executive to the assembly line supervisor, would implement a few of these management principles, even some routine jobs would not be boring.

Even if your boss is an insensitive bully and your job routine, there is something you yourself can do. Boredom probably has as much to do with one's attitude as with duties.

The authors' son, Philip, explained the situation to them.

"When I was working the sorting line at UPS, I hated the job. That night shift after a day of classes was a killer. But some nights were better than others. Some nights I'd say to myself, 'I am going to really move those packages tonight.' I would get fired up about the job and it wouldn't be bad at all. But the nights I went in thinking about what a hard, backbreaking, boring job it was, I had a long miserable night."

Injecting Interest

Most jobs can be made interesting with the use of a little imagination. If not, the people with whom we work can be interesting. If there isn't anything interesting about the job or the people at work, then you will probably find that people at home are not very interesting either. You are bored with life.

One solution to boredom is described by David Conover in *One Man's Island.* He wrote, "In making love, or making a dessert, I am the constant novice. When I am not learning I know I am not living. The tragedy of life is our inability to grow, to change, to stretch. Each day beckons me to enlarge myself."[5]

Keeping a goal before us, trying to learn something new, if not on the job then about the family or a hobby, keeps us alive.

Alexander Reid Martin, a Manhattan psychoanalyst, has a prescription for avoiding boredom.[6] He suggests:

—Develop the courage to show your natural feelings. Find someone to tell your troubles to.

—Use the resources of your mind—imagination, contemplation, and recollection—to arouse enthusiasm to replace boredom.

—Respect your real self, not an image of yourself which you feel will be more acceptable to people important to you.

These suggestions are more principles than specific methods for change, but they point us in the right direction.

In *Learn to Grow Old,* Paul Tournier speaks to retirement age boredom:

> Inquiries among retired people clearly indicate what that [much leisure time] may lead to: Regression, boredom, and even anxiety-neurosis.
>
> What each of us needs is a "reconversion" from earning a living to cultural activity. So long as we talk only of the use of leisure, we seem to be suggesting that all that matters is to find the means of killing time without getting too bored. To acquire culture, however, is something different—it is to develop oneself, to progress, to contribute to the progress of the human race, to find meaning in life which can survive the cessation of professional activity.[7]

In his excellent book on life planning, *The Three Boxes of Life,* Richard N. Bolles suggests: "Forget how old you are and keep on planning—just as though you're going to keep on living. The one thing that keeps you going is to have an objective. You should have ambitions, and work to fulfill them. Then you can forget about actuarial tables and life expectancy statistics."[8]

Life must have its rewards for us to maintain interest and energy. If the job is not interesting then our leisure activities must be. Though some of those activities may contain competitive sports or specific objectives or goals, some of them should be playful in nature. As Judi Balley wrote, "If done in an 'easy-does-it' manner, self-improvement is certainly no neurotic goal. But if all leisure involves proving yourself, little freedom, relaxation, or harmony will be gained."[9]

Another Summer Coming

In *Twilight Zone: The Movie,* people are depicted in a nursing home wasting away. No hope, no smiles, no life in that home. The late Scatman Crothers shows up to teach them how to start enjoying life even though their circumstances seem hopeless. At one point he says, "When you stop playing, you start dying. You need another summer, another game to look forward to."

We cannot wait for a Scatman Crothers to solve our problem of boredom for us. We have to take charge and do it for ourselves.

What kind of reward do you want out of life?

A new hobby?

An exciting project through your church?

A special vacation?

A new vocation?

A new skill?

Whatever your choice is, the chances are that when you become excited about something new, or a new way of looking at something "old" (spouse, children, job) that the people near to you will catch the feel for that new aliveness and other areas of life will seem less boring too.

12

The Dignity of Work and Play

The brilliant novelist Herman Melville wrote, "They talk of the dignity of work. Bosh! The dignity is in leisure." That is not a very brilliant statement. Melville followed the Greek idea of leisure.

The Greeks equated leisure with contemplative and intellectual insights. They would not have understood our highly work-oriented way of life. To them, happiness was found in leisure. The capacity to use leisure creatively was the basis of free people's whole life. Work found its meaning in relation to leisure.

The Greek split-level society of seers and slaves, thinkers and laborers, royalty and servitude would naturally wrestle with this problem and come out on the side of leisure. Socrates proclaimed that "Leisure is the best of all possessions."

In the classic work on play, *Homo Ludens,* Johan Huizinga writes, "For many years the conviction has grown upon me that civilization arises and unfolds in and as play . . . . Play is to be understood here not as a biological phenomenon but as a cultural phenomenon."[1] Huizinga is half right, because culture certainly influences the forms play takes and expresses its culture, but it is also a biological phenomenon.

The Greek culture idolized leisure and play and minimized work, whereas American culture would tend to idolize work and minimize leisure. Cultural influences determine the difference between the two societies.

The Dignity in Work

In our culture there is dignity in work. Ask George, who worked for over twenty years at a steel mill, about the dignity of work. He was laid off two years ago. Ask him how he feels about standing in food stamp lines and living on "welfare."

Ask Rachel, the single parent of a teenage son and former advertising executive, how it feels to be out of work. Ask Lacy, a former top executive with an engineering firm before the ownership changed, how it feels to look for a job for six months, while having to say "no" to almost every request his children make. Watch him try to explain to Lacy, Jr., why he cannot go to soccer camp. Ask Tom and Teresa how it feels to lose the farm after it's been in the family for four generations.

There is dignity in work. The job does not have to be prestigious or on the top of the pay scale, but most people in our culture need to work to feel worthy. Most people need a reason to get up in the morning. There has to be meaning to life, and work supports that feeling of meaning. When there is not any work, the job we sometimes gripe about so much seems like the end of the rainbow.

There is dignity in work. The dignity may not be in the nature of the job. It may be in the fact that a person supports a family, can respond to the church's plea to help feed the hungry and care for those who cannot find work. There is dignity in work when people know that what they do with their money does good for others.

The same people who complain about not having enough time to play find it almost impossible to enjoy the forced leisure that comes from being out of work. That leisure is not renewing, because there is not the balance of work to give additional meaning to life.

The dignity of work lies not in the product but in the person. The papal encyclical *Laborem Exeacens* puts the person at the center of work when it says, "The basis for determining the value of human work is not primarily the kind of work being done but the fact that the one who is doing it is a person . . . . In the first place work is for the person and not the person for work."[2]

There is dignity in work because people bring their sense of worth to the job. Work is an expression of our worth, it does not create our worth. Except for those who have been taught from childhood that one should not have to work, a person out of work feels guilty and suffers diminishing self-esteem.

There is dignity in work because it enables people to demonstrate their skills, apply their energies to something that makes a difference, and use the resulting money to express their values.

The Dignity of Leisure

The dignity of leisure is the other side of the coin of the dignity of work. The dignity of leisure lies not in the activity but in the person. We bring our worth to the time and place and play the silly game or watch a setting sun close the day and are renewed, refreshed, and re-energized.

Dr. Richard Harrison, friend and colleague, captured the thought in a letter to Loren. After suggesting an article pertaining to the subject, he wrote:

> It seems to me that what you believe is that play in its various forms provides re-creation so that mentally and physically and spiritually we might go on about our creative tasks in the world.
>
> In other words, unlike many of the writers on play a

few years ago, you would not disparage work. Rather, you see work and play as a part of the whole of life, neither isolated from the other.

The fine line between work and play becomes even more blurred when we realize that play is more an attitude than an activity. After Thomas Edison had worked sixteen hours a day, seven days a week for months, Mrs. Edison said to her husband, "You must go on a vacation. You have worked long enough without rest. Decide which place you would rather be than anywhere else in the world and go there."

Edison replied, "I'll go there tomorrow."

The next day, Edison returned to the laboratory.

Evidently, Edison enjoyed playing with ideas and inventions. A forced vacation would have produced irritation and anxiety instead of rest and relaxation for him.

Three Ways to Work and Play

There are three basic ways people apply themselves to work and play. Some people work at work and play playfully. Others work at both work and play. Still others play at working and play playfully. The latter follow the advice, "It isn't work if you wouldn't rather be someplace else." That is true only if people approach work with a playful, exciting attitude. There are those who escape into their work to avoid the boredom of leisure or to compensate for some psychological need. The escapists may rather work than play to avoid a hostile marriage or to try to demonstrate just how much suffering they can endure. These compulsive collectors of vocational victories expend all their energies in working and are candidates for emotional and physical illness.

Robert Neale touches on this idea when he writes, "The individual who sees himself consistently as one at play in the world is expressing his state of inner harmony . . . . Play is psychologically defined as any activity not motivated by the need to resolve inner conflict."[3]

In our culture, living the rhythm of life, balancing all the parts of work and play, time and tasks, family and finances is not easy. In the midst of all the pressures, one can identify with the words from *The Hotel New Hampshire:* "It's hard work and great art to make life not so serious."

For most people in our culture the art of play is the most difficult to learn. John Erskine summarizes the problem.

> Leisure . . . freedom to do what we like . . . is the most difficult of arts . . . [because it involves] an obligation to be what we are not yet, to become on the creative side of character whatever is possible for us . . . mere amusements and diversions [do not satisfy . . . they] are not sufficiently creative. The true use of leisure is to produce something characteristic of ourselves, to project our personalities, to stretch our souls.[4]

Play Takes Practice

After attending classes all morning, Philip was tired and did not "feel like doing anything," he said. Instead of going to the library, he dropped by two college friends' apartment. Ronnie was lying on the couch half asleep, while Larry's loose body slouched in the large lounge chair. When Philip entered the room, both men lazily lifted their heads to acknowledge Philip's presence.

"That sure looks like a good time," Philip said. "I wish I could lie around like that doing nothing when I had a lot to do."

"It takes a lot of practice," Ronnie said. "It's an art. You don't have it mastered until you can lie around all day and not feel guilty about it. Otherwise you don't get anything done and you don't get any R & R either."

Ronnie emphasized the principle that wherever you are and whatever you are doing, to benefit from the activity you must live in the present—to be receptive to the experience available. This does not imply perpetual play as demonstrated by Dan Kiley in *The Peter Pan Syndrome.* He shows where Peter Pan people who play all the time experience irresponsibility, anxiety, loneliness, sex role conflicts, and eventually become fatalistic and irrational while indulging in magical thinking. Kiley writes, "There's certainly nothing wrong with having the desire to join Peter and his frivolous fellows. Nothing, that is, provided you return from never-never land when it's time to deal with the real world." We agree with Kiley except we think that Peter Pan's playfulness is part of our real world. In a sense Kiley thinks so too, as expressed in the following words: "Peter Pan symbolizes the essence of youthfulness. The joy. The indefatigable spirit . . . . He awakens the child in us. We are drawn to him . . . . When we allow Peter Pan to touch our heart, our soul is nourished by the fountain of youth."[5]

Play: An Attitude toward Life

Play is essentially an attitude toward all life—work and play, family and friends, church and career. When there is an absence of inner conflict we are peacefully present and that is renewing whether we call it work or play.

This is not to imply that some leisure activities cannot be used solely to relieve tension and temporarily resolve inner conflict.

Mel explained, "Every Saturday I play golf. Every Friday night and Saturday morning before tee time, I fantasize a great game of golf. I picture the ball sailing off the first tee straight down the fairway, see my seven iron shot bite the green and stop six feet from the hole. I sink the putt. *But* when I play, the ball slices, I shank my irons, and miss most putts. I curse the ball as if it intentionally dodges the hole. When I get home and Carol asks me how I did, it makes me even madder."

In spite of the potentially hazardous fallout, that leisure activity probably does something for Mel. For one thing, it helps him appreciate the office where he is partially in control of inanimate objects such as memos, machines, and mail. On the golf course, Mel trades one kind of inner conflict for a less serious form of tension, that is, unless he has a heart problem.

Mel could benefit by listening to Matthew Kelty.

> "We like it if you listen to music and play some. We like it if you notice rain, feel the wind, hear the birds, smell the soap. We like to be awake, not asleep; alive not dead; in touch not gone . . . . If there are monsters in our depths, and there are, there is also the presence of God."[6]

To follow Kelty's advice is a real art that for most of us will require much practice. For play is more than action, it is an attitude that pervades all life.

13

Choosing Your Play

A recent survey on small business stress reported in the "Harvard Business Review" revealed that most of the executives surveyed loved their work. However, about two-thirds of the 450 executives studied admitted suffering from back problems, indigestion, insomnia, or headaches which they related to job stress.

These people find their work challenging. They would rather be at work than anywhere else, yet suffer because they do not play. One would guess that their work suffers from their stranglehold on it and themselves.

For those small business executives who were brave enough to take a holiday, the results were usually worthwhile. One individual, who had constant indigestion which prevented him from sleeping despite the regular use of antacids, found that his symptoms completely disappeared while on a vacation in Germany despite a diet of Bavarian sausages and other delicacies—definitely not part of an ulcer diet.

This and other research suggests that a properly

planned sabbatical, holiday, or vacation can do wonders for us.

In an interview, the very talented actor Jack Nicholson said, "I've always had fun working with stimulating people. But I always felt a little angry that I had to get up at 8:00 every morning, and I had been doing it for three years. I felt drained. So I decided to quit for awhile and let the old well fill up again . . . . I enjoyed not having a schedule. I read some, wrote some, rode some. It was a great sabbatical."

Though Jack enjoyed his work, he felt drained. And as in every job there was at least one thing that irritated him. He needed a sabbatical. He needed to step back, view his life, and "Let the old well fill up." He did not do nothing. He read, wrote, and rode.

The Value of a Sabbatical

A recent government survey found that fourteen percent of the nation's white-collar workers are employed by companies now offering some form of sabbatical program. A sabbatical does not imply lifelessness; it suggests that the person is being renewed in some way by doing something different in a place other than his or her normal work arena. "Since 1971, IBM has allowed employees to take social service leaves, with full IBM pay, to volunteer at nonprofit community organizations. More than 600 IBMers have been loaned to local community organizations, and some 500 more to educational institutions through faculty loan programs."[1]

We may not be privileged to take a one-month or one-year sabbatical to renew ourselves, but we can take mini-sabbaticals called weekend holidays and vacations. But to benefit from our sabbatical, we need the playful attitude. In his insightful book, *Human Options,* Norman Cousins warns:

> There is the inactivity that restores, of course, but isn't there also the inactivity that destroys through withdrawal and decay? What about the person who doesn't know the

> difference between relaxation and lifelessness? Obviously, total rest and inactivity may be essential ingredients of relaxation for certain people under certain circumstances at certain times; but it should be equally obvious that immobility is not quite the same as serenity, a state of inaction is not the same as a state of grace.[2]

In a state of grace we do not feel inner conflict; we experience inner harmony. We are at peace with ourselves. A sabbatical, holiday, and vacation should lead to a state of grace. Unfortunately, many do not.

For people who are too busy and think they do not have time to take a sabbatical, holiday, vacation, or a day off from work Charles Swindoll suggests the following.[3]

—a quote: "Much of our activity these days is nothing more than a cheap anesthetic to deaden the pain of an empty life."

—A four-point plan:

1. Admit that you are too busy. Say it to yourself, your family, and your friends. [Confess, don't brag; bragging about how busy we are usually implies that we are very important people. Confessing suggests that a change is needed.]
2. Stop saying yes to every request. Practice saying no.
3. Maintain this practice. It is easy to try saying "no" for a few weeks and then slip back into your charming ways. Swindoll writes, "Discuss with your family some ways of investing time with them—without TV . . . without apologies for playing and laughing and doing nutty, fun things."
4. Share it. Tell others how much fun you are having since deciding to stop being too busy to start living.

The Problem of Structured Play

It takes determination and planning to play playfully, for there are many other obstacles waiting to spoil our renewal plans. Our culture tries to force us to play according to the internal rules of our social station. The bone-crushing pro football player, Rosie Grier, doing needlepoint is news worth a commercial (football players are not supposed to do needlepoint to relax, but who's going to tell him?). The bank executive is supposed to play golf, enjoy quarter horses, and maybe play tennis. When her hobby is drag racing, that is news. Blue-collar workers are supposed to play in the softball league, bowling league, and go fishing and hunting. When one of them shows an interest in bird-watching, landscape painting and poetry, that is news. Some people must go to Vail, Colorado, skiing whether they like it or not.

Because of social expectations, many people are subtly "forced" to use their leisure in a way less than satisfying. People are supposed to play according to their age. When someone sixty years old does anything but a slow foxtrot on the dance floor, others stare at the "jitterbuggers" as if they had committed a crime.

Playing Playfully

One obstacle to many people being free enough to let themselves play playfully is the fear of being embarrassed. Embarrassment is caused by not conforming—by doing that which society says we should not do. We are judged against some norm of behavior or appearance that we and others have agreed upon, consciously or unconsciously. The social pressure is supposed to keep us in line with the unwritten rules. People think, "I don't want to embarrass myself by saying the wrong thing or wearing the wrong thing—or doing the wrong thing." Some people are humiliated if they use the wrong fork for their salad at the dinner party. Others are so afraid of appearing stupid, they do not enter into the conversation at the party. Others are embarrassed beyond words for wearing the wrong clothes to the event. None of these people will enjoy themselves, will play at the party. Why? Because they are still worrying about what others think about them. There is no way they can play while concentrating on their appearance, manners, and demeanor.

In the late 1940s a few of the brothers of the Phi Delta Theta fraternity on the University of Florida campus decided to play a practical joke on Homer. Homer, a freshman, was just off the farm. The fraternity planned a "hoedown" farm theme for the Frolics. Everyone else was dressing in overalls, plaid shirts, bandanas, and straw hats. The practical jokers invited Homer to the party, rented him a tuxedo, and dressed him formally for the occasion. They were expecting Homer to be embarrassed. He wasn't. Homer enjoyed the special attention and exploited the situation to its fullest. He had more fun than anyone.

We have to be willing to be embarrassed to be so. We have to accept others' rules for living before we can be humiliated. Or we have to violate our rules publicly to pass judgment on ourselves.

All embarrassment is experienced as inferiority. Homer did not feel inferior though others tried to publicly expose what they considered his inferior social graces.

The authors are not suggesting we all violate the rituals that help groups maintain identity. We are suggesting that when the rules force us to be so self-conscious we do not play, it is time to declare our independence. We need then to play playfully in a way that puts us in touch with our inner harmony. To do otherwise is to betray ourselves.

The running (jogging) guru and physician, George Sheehan, observed: "Play is the path to self-knowledge, the way to self-acceptance. If you would know yourself and then accept that knowledge, you must first find your play, and learn to play."[4]

What Is Your Play?

The following list of activities gleaned from letters, questionnaires, and in seminars may help you choose a form of play most suitable to your inner way of doing life rather than the socially accepted play forms:

Music—listening to
—singing in a choir
—playing an instrument
Visiting friends
Golf
Tennis
Bowling
Fishing (all types)
Racquetball
Soccer
Football
Baseball (softball)
Running
Swimming
Bicycling
Volleyball
Wrestling (playfully)
Roller-skating
Hot tubbing
Reading
Visiting with family
Needlepoint
Latch hook projects
Crossword puzzles
Playing piano
Picnics
Sex
Working with spouse on house projects
Crocheting
Cooking out
Family camping
Flying
Exercising to jazz records
Skeet shooting
Meditation—time for solitude
Writing articles and books
Jigsaw puzzles
Computer programming
Floral arrangements
Napping
Umpiring baseball
Laughing
Motorcycling
Walking in the snow
Billiards
Preaching
Automobile mechanics
Housecleaning
Cross-stitch
Video games
Fantasize
Walking in woods—Hiking
Daily walks
Painting
Playing cards
Carving
Attending movies
Dining out
Sightseeing
Flying kites
Table games
Chess
Sewing
Television
Window shopping
People watching
Sleigh riding
Ice skating
Canoeing
Going to church
Theatre
Concerts
Gardening
Joking
Dancing

Traveling
Hunting
Collecting coins
Stamp collecting
Mowing the lawn
Craftwork
Spectator sports
Browsing bookstores
Browsing hardware stores
Visiting museums
Writing poetry
Drawing
Designing
Driving
Reading newspapers
Bee keeping
Playing with a pet
Hook rugs
Baking goodies
Ping-pong
Quilting
Model trains
Model airplanes
Writing in a journal
Knitting

It is obvious that most of these adults are finding ways to renew themselves at one level or another. What has been stated before is equally obvious: What is play for some people is work for others, and the opposite is also true.

If you are not being renewed by your play, maybe you are responding to social pressure and need to do what you really want to regularly. For sabbaticals, holidays, and vacations may come in mini-packages of time—a weekend, a day, an hour. The length of time is not as important as the attitude we assume when we play.

An assembly line worker expressed it beautifully. She said, "When the pressure builds or the monotony starts to get to me, I take a little vacation by singing gospel songs softly when I work. The other workers don't seem to mind, and after about fifteen minutes of singing, I'm back on top of the world."

What is your way to get back on top of the world?

Play Like a Child

Our friend Walter Johnson, a great player, offers an explanation that helps summarize attitudes toward play.

> I have two types of people I fish with. The first type is going to catch fish. These people study weather signs, moon positions, water temperature, and read books and articles on fishing. Every conceivable type bait is prepared—live minnows, rubber worms, and several dozen artificial lures. The boat is pampered, the food bagged, and cooler filled. With a vengeance, these people attack the lake and fish. Through gritted teeth they cast the lure to the bass and dare them not to strike. Fishing is war, filled with all the emotion of life-or-death issues.
>
> *We catch fish!* And I'm exhausted but satisfied. No doubt about it, that kind of fishing is work, but it produces trophies to put on the wall and bragging rights at work. I enjoy the challenge. It is a type of renewal for me.
>
> The second type of people with whom I fish approach the opportunity in an entirely different way. They may check to see if a tornado is forecast, but no chart reading. They carry the appropriate bait and may examine their

> equipment. Lazily, we enter the boat and drift about the lake half hoping a fish will find the bait alluring. We eat, talk, and laugh until a fish disturbs our peaceful day. If we catch fish, that's a bonus. If we don't, so what? While enjoying the beauty of nature, we have a relaxing, enjoyable visit with each other.

The first type of people may need that kind of activity if they have boring jobs. However, if their work is filled with tension-producing challenges and if they approach their work as they do their fishing, they need some leisure activity that can relax them while they are playing. They do not need to work at catching fish.

The second type of people are playing and this form of fishing may be exactly what they need, especially if they have challenging, tension-filled jobs. They play at fishing. In his popular book, *Confessions of a Workaholic,* Dr. Wayne Oates counsels, "Rest, leisure, laziness is necessary for the maintenance, sustenance and renewal of the balanced life. Yet it must come individually prescribed, in carefully matched doses, depending upon a careful study of your and my work—play, play-rest rhythm."[1]

No one can tell anyone else how to play—how to renew, refresh, and re-energize themselves, but some ideas may help us discover our unique way to do it.

Basic Characteristics of Play

As a checklist for you, we will list the basic characteristics of play. Evaluate your leisure activities against the criteria to determine whether you are playing with or working at your leisure time.

1. *Lost in the activity.* Time stands still. You are totally present emotionally, intellectually, physically and spiritually. You do not feel guilty or fearful, anxious or lonely. In fact, you are not consciously aware of yourself doing anything. You are not self-conscious.

2. *No criteria for success.* You are not trying to prove anything to yourself or anyone else. The justification for

the activity is inherent in the activity itself. It is worthy of our time without having to be useful, especially the resolving of inner conflict, or the collecting of another trophy.

3. *Freely chosen.* You are not being coerced or forced or pressured in any way to participate in this activity. You have chosen to use your leisure time in this way because you think it will be fun.

4. *Spontaneous.* When "doing" the activity you feel free inside and spontaneously enjoy the time and activity. You break the rules and regulations that usually confine your feelings, thoughts, and actions. The activity evokes a childlike quality in you.

5. *Feel a deep joy and internal unity.* While playing you have a sense of well-being, a feeling of being in touch with something both inside and yet bigger than you are. This feeling cannot be explained in words. As Louis Armstrong, the jazz musician, is credited with saying, "Rhythm is what if you've got it, you don't need a definition; and if you don't got it, no definition is any good." His play was music and in his response to how jazz music feels he described a quality of play for all of us.

The experience defies definition yet the Bible has a word for it—*joy.* This joy comes from feeling in union with ourselves and with God or the universe. We somehow sense that we are a part of and participating in the divine/human drama. Robert K. Johnston describes the phenomenon succinctly, "By allowing us to transcend ourselves and enter a new time and space, play can become the avenue through which God communes with us . . . . It is enough to suggest that in play God can, and often does, meet us and commune with us." God gives us the gift of joy even when we do not recognize or acknowledge God's presence.

Play and Peace

When real play occurs we can appreciate the words of Isaiah 55:12, ". . . you shall go out with joy, and be led forth with peace." Because we cannot program God and cannot totally control what happens to us and how we will feel when it does, we cannot always play playfully and have this experience of inner harmony—of joy. We can increase the probability of such experiences by learning new ways of attitudes toward play.

Jesus' reference to and use of a child gives us direction again. "Truly, I say to you, unless you turn and become like children, you will never enter the kingdom of heaven. Whoever humbles himself like this child, he is the greatest in the kingdom of heaven" (Matthew 18:3).

The word "turn" implies, "Return to the Source of Life." To turn in this sense is to recapture the joy and spontaneity of childhood that has been trampled on by fears, resentments, and a host of other repressive forces which keep our childlikeness imprisoned. To turn is to return to that holy intimacy created within us, which enables us to experience the presence of God.

The kingdom of heaven is a phrase interchangeable with the kingdom of God. The kingdom of God literally means the place where God resides and rules. So anyplace God rules is the kingdom of God. This does not simply mean some time in the future; but whenever and wherever God is present the kingdom of heaven is there. So to experience God's presence, to feel that joy of union, to be free of inner conflict, we must recapture the essence of childlikeness.

Recapturing Renewal

We will list the characteristics that may enable us to recapture this special renewing quality.

1. *Whoever humbles himself like a child.* The word "humble" does not mean self-effacing, groveling behavior. It has nothing to do with the characteristics manifested by those people who are proud of their sin, brag about their unworthiness, and exploit their "humble" nature. To be humble is to be awed by the world, to realize how much there is to see, smell, touch, hear, and learn. To be humble is to become aware there is much more to know, to experience, and to perceive than we can ever imagine.

To be humble is also to realize we are dependent on God and interdependent with people. We cannot do life joyously alone. To return to a state of childlikeness is not returning to a helpless type of dependency, which is a neurotic regression to leaving life's decisions to others. It is not the shirking of adult responsibility. It is a return to the created calm unity within, which gives us the energy and insight to be more responsibly alive *with* others.

2. *Trusting people and God like a child.* Until life roughs them up too much, children trust people and the world. This trust frees them to venture into unknown territory and to explore uncharted courses in their families, with their friends, and through their small world. They see what adults seldom see—the yellow and black and red butterfly, the clouds that look like horses and mountains, their reflection in the pond. Children can turn a pot into a drum, a bag of trash into three toys, and a stick into a boat. Children watch worms crawl and wonder how they can do it without legs. Children ask questions about bugs and birth, dustballs and death. They are awed by the daisy growing out of a stone wall and the dog with three legs. Children see and feel the family conflict and often act like they don't. They see the love and laughter and want in on it.

To return to childlikeness is to become awed by the world about us and start seeing that which is worth seeing. It is to take our eyes off the bank balance and professional priorities to notice the living that is begging to be seen and experienced.

It is a shame that we sometimes have to be jarred back to our senses by tragedy. The person who faces death and barely escapes often begins to notice ordinary things. At times the person recovering from a heart attack becomes humorous in commenting on the previously unnoticed beauty of life.

"Look at the sunset. Have you ever seen anything so beautiful?"

"Junior, can we play for a little while? Do you have time?"

"Have you ever noticed how salt sparkles?"

"Thank you so much for fixing dinner. The hotdog was gourmet."

"Look at the shape of the leaves on that oak tree. And the acorns. Aren't acorns interesting? Such big trees grow from such small things."

As adults we do not have time to explore every acorn, yet we can be open to the experiences that life offers us. We can begin to adventure into a few uncharted courses and trust God to make it interesting. The fact is life is always interesting; it is our perception that needs honing. With the open, adventuresome spirit we learn to play playfully and experience the joy that renews.

3. *Being candid—honest like a child.* Children have to be taught to conceal their thoughts and hide their feelings. Before they learn that lesson they are free to (and often do) say what is on their minds and openly express their love, cry when they hurt, and act angry when they are. Because they are not confined by unnecessary do's and do nots, musts and must nots, they are open to the stimulation that comes into their arena of life. Of course, their honesty often shocks adults.

When Loren was about eighteen years old, he, his mother and father, and one brother were visiting in the living room. Ten-year-old Jackie, a next door neighbor, walked into the living room to visit. A few minutes later, Loren's grandmother walked through the front door like a model, wearing a new pink and pastel blue dress, blue medium-heeled shoes, a matching handbag, and a pastel blue hat with tiny pink roses decorating the wide brim.

Mrs. Broadus was clearly impressed with her new outfit. She looked in the mirror, adjusted her hat a little and received the compliments graciously. Then she turned to Jackie and asked, "How old do you think I am, Jackie?"

Taking the challenge seriously, Jackie looked at Mrs. Broadus's body, then her face, and said, "At least a hundred."

Mrs. Broadus left the house without saying a word.

Adults probably should not be that honest with others over insignificant issues (of course, it wasn't insignificant to Mrs. Broadus). We need to be honest with ourselves. We must be open to our needs to change that in us which prevents us from experiencing the rhythm of life—the joy and the pain, the love and the laughter, the work and the play.

When we recapture the childlike qualities we will experience the joy in our play and maybe in our work. We will learn to play for our life in a spontaneous, humble, trusting, joyous way and feel our worth as a part of God's creation.

Then we will "go out with joy, and be led forth with peace."

15

Laughter As Play

Laughter has become big business and is gaining in popularity every day. Bob Greene, the *Chicago Tribune* columnist, reported on a consulting firm that teaches top executives how to use humor. "Businessmen and businesswomen want to have a good sense of humor badly," said Malcolm Kushner, a partner in Golden Gates writers. "They may be the smartest, most aggressive executives in town—but if they know they aren't funny, it makes them miserable." The purpose of the seminars is to teach people to "speak to people with a little warmth and humor, then those people will be more receptive to listening to them."

Let us hope that the firm is successful, because it is usually a sad scene when a humorless person tries to be funny by telling a joke. The humorless person is miserable, because without the joy and elation of laughter life is one serious, tension-filled roller coaster of good and bad decisions. People who cannot occasionally laugh at their failures and mock their successes are doomed to a miserable life. The premise of the humor seminars is: If you help people laugh and relax, they forget their problems long enough to listen to someone else.

Making Room for Laughter

Laughter has become big business. In a hospital near Atlanta, Georgia, there is a "laughing room" in which patients are encouraged to watch funny movies, read funny books, and play with assorted items. The purpose is to help people get well through laughter. The hospital reports that the laughing room decreases people's need for pain medication and serves as an antidepressant.

Norman Cousins started a happy revolution when he published *Anatomy of an Illness.*[1] From personal experience and through interviews with others, he demonstrated that laughter can be a therapeutic aid in overcoming illness. Laughter, and the positive attitudes required by it, release tension, can affect the cardiovascular system, stimulate endorphins in the brain, which are natural painkillers, and promote other health-enhancing effects. Following Cousins' book, laughter became a serious subject of study not only for professional comedians, but for physicians, philosophers, psychologists, sociologists, theologians, and all those professionally interested in people. This promotion of laughter is an encouraging sign because of the physical, emotional, and spiritual renewal that comes with laughing. Laughter has been and still is in some circles considered a weakness in character and a saboteur of commitment to serious causes.

A professional consultant conducting a management symposium explained how he almost did not get his Ph.D. When the Ph.D. committee met, he stood his orals with each professor questioning him in detail about his dissertation, and then the distinguished professors discussed his qualifications, character, and intelligence in closed session. One stately gentleman said, "I'm suspicious of David. He seems to be laughing and having a good time all the time."

The implication, of course, was if you're having a good time instructing you must not be qualified to teach this serious subject.

This professor must have taken Plato too seriously. Plato warned his guardians of the ideal state not to be given to laughter, for "violent laughter tends to provoke an equally violent reaction." Plato knew that laughter questions authority which must control by fear, for laughter can be "resistance to authority and an escape from its pressure; and its mechanism is a free discharge of repressed energy or resentment through laughter."[2] Jürgen Moltmann writes, "Games, jokes, caricatures, parodies, imitations, and intentional misunderstandings may be regarded as a means of emancipation for those who are burdened and heavy-laden. The medieval dances of death served to liberate the people by denuding the privileged classes of their trappings of dignity and their status symbols."[3] Maybe that is why Lord Chesterfield wrote, "In my mind there is nothing so ill-bred as audible laughter."

When people are repressed or controlled by others in such a way as to create resentment, laughter is a temporary break for freedom—the equalizer of all people and the release from inner tension, at least temporarily.

Looking at Laughter

Humor, laughter, comedy—all have been "big business" for philosophers, prophets, comedians, and clowns. A few quotes will give some range of people's interest and ideas.

"Man is the only creature endowed with the power of laughter; is he not also the only one that deserves to be laughed at?" *Fulke Greville.*

"A laugh is worth a hundred groans in any market." *Charles Lamb.*

"Man alone suffers so excruciatingly in the world that he was compelled to invent laughter." *Friedrich W. Nietzche.*

"The young man who has not wept is a savage, and the old man who will not laugh is a fool." *George Santayana.*

"A laugh, to be joyous, must flow from a joyous heart, for without kindness there can be no true joy." *Thomas Carlyle.*

"The most utterly lost of all days is that in which you have not once laughed." *Sebastien Rock Nicholas Chamfort.*

"Equipped with the anti-toxin of laughter, one can live even in a standardized society without being too impressed by its standards." *Irwin Edman.*

"Men show their character in nothing more clearly than by what they find laughable." *Johann W. Von Goethe.*

"Laughter is the sensation of feeling good all over, and showing it principally in one spot." *Bob Hope* and *Josh Billings.*

"No society is in good health without laughing at itself quietly and privately." *Wylie Sypher.*

"What I want to do is to make people laugh so that they'll see things seriously." *William K. Zinsser.*

"A man who can smile when things go wrong has found someone to blame it on." *Lawrence J. Peter.*

"Laughter is the shortest distance between two people." *Victor Borge.*

"The art of medicine consists of amusing the patient while nature cures the disease." *Voltaire.*

"It [laughter] is, come to think of it, an absolute necessity in the maintenance of sanity." *Steve Allen.*

"Laugh at yourself first, before anyone else can." *Elsa Maxwell.*

"Humor is the sense of the absurd which is despair refusing to take itself seriously." *Arland Ussher.*

"Life does not cease to be funny when people die anymore than it ceases to be serious when people laugh." *George Bernard Shaw.*

"I have always felt sorry for people afraid of feeling, of sentimentality, who are unable to weep with their whole heart because those who do not know how to weep, do not know how to laugh either." *Golda Meir.*

"The comic appeals to the intellect pure and simple; laughter is incompatible with emotion." *Henri Bergson.*

"Laughter is the result of an expectation which, of a sudden, ends in nothing." *Herbert Spenser.*

"Just as 'free association' is never free, but is governed and guided by emotions ordinarily repressed, so humor is the unwitting messenger of truths that churn behind a camouflage of levity." *Leo Rosten.*

"A sense of humor has been connected with longevity. Those who laugh often, tradition says, live long." *Tom Mullen.*

"You grow up the day you have the first real laugh at yourself." *Ethel Barrymore.*

The quotes could go on for pages, but the preceding offers an overview of the ways laughter is used to renew people. Obviously, some of these people are having trouble finding anything humorous about life, while others are learning and laughing a lot.

Renewal through Laughter

We will select a few themes that pertain to renewal through laughter.

As in play, laughter is a break from taking ourselves too seriously. We are "lost" in the act of laughing; we do not think about ourselves. The sudden surprise ending to a joke, or the unexpected comment jars loose our tight grip on the world, and we explode in laughter. The muscles relax, the tension spews out, and the mind lets it happen. As Milton Berle said, "Laughter is a minute vacation." The belly laugh may hurt so much that we beg for mercy—"Stop! Stop! My stomach is aching too much." Norman Cousins called this kind of laughter "internal jogging." After the limp feeling, people usually have more energy than before the laughing spell.

Joel Goodman, who conducts seminars on "The Role of Love and Laughter in the Healing Process," believes that the average American laughs fifteen times a day. When told this, one person said, "The people I work with must be hilarious at home," which is a sad commentary on any organization.

In *The Book of Laughter and Forgetting,* the Czechoslovakian novelist, Milan Kundera, described our need for this therapy through his characters.

"Laughter? Does anyone ever care about laughter? I mean real laughter—beyond jokes, jeering, ridicule. Laughter—delight unbounded, delight delectable, delight of delights . . . .

"I said to my sister or she said to me, come let's play laughter together. We stretched out side by side on the bed and started in. At first we just made believe, of course. Forced laughs. Laughable laughs. Laughs so laughable they made us laugh. Then it came—real laughter, total laughter—sweeping us off in unbounded effusion. Bursts of laughter, laughter rehashed, jostled laughter, laughter defleshed, magnificent laughter, sumptuous and wild . . . and we laughed to the infinity of the laughter of our laughs . . . . O laughter! Laughter at delight, delight of laughter. Laughing deeply is living deeply."[4]

Laughter: Key to Survival

Sad is the person who suppresses that kind of laughter. The capacity to laugh at our absurdity—the foolish mistakes, the times we get upset over things that aren't really important are related to our capacity to survive joyously, and some say to survive for long either emotionally, physically, or spiritually.

It is regrettable that we teach children not to laugh, instead of honing their skills at perceiving the humorous. We teach them to be vain, serious about unimportant issues—to conceal their feelings, and to be careful when they laugh. That is not natural for children and other living people.

A friend's daughter, Jennifer Barr and her nine-year-old chum, Donna, were sitting on the living room floor playing a board game. Jennifer made her move and the two girls giggled. Her friend made her move and they giggled again. As the game and ritual continued, the giggling increased, each time a little longer than the last time. Finally Jennifer said, "Let's stop playing the game and just giggle." So they did.

It is not natural for adults to block out of their minds, emotions, and bodies the joy of laughter. Vanity often prevents us from seeing the humor in our absurdity.

The story is told about Freud making a house call on an ill woman. He examined the woman, turned to the husband and whispered, "I don't like the way she looks."

The man replied, "I don't either, but what can I do about it?" The incongruity in this situation gives some people a minute vacation.

Three young women in their seventies took a ninety-two-year-old friend to a special luncheon. When the very young waitress approached the table, one of the distinguished women said, "Today is Elsie's ninety-second birthday. Bring her a special dessert."

"Which one is Elsie?" asked the waitress.

What a compliment to Elsie! And if the other three ladies were perceptive to the situation, they could have enjoyed it more.

We may not live or work with people who express their sense of humor freely. If we do not have a healthy dose of laughter almost every day in our family relations, the family is in trouble. For it is as important for a family to play and to laugh together as it is to work and pray together. If our working relations are strained, someone should find ways to help people laugh together.

Laughter: Door to Renewal

We offer a few suggestions for renewing yourself through laughter:

1. Find and cultivate a friend or two with whom you can laugh regularly and occasionally "stop playing the game and just laugh" uncontrollably. As one vivacious young woman said, "I know how to play. All I need is someone to do it with."

2. Use lunch time to relax, play, and laugh. One of the worst practices ever instituted is the working lunch, at which people stuff food in their mouths while their minds work full speed on major decisions and manipulative methods. Have lunch with someone you enjoy and have a few laughs while savoring the salad.

The exercise lunch break is catching on. Instead of eating during the lunch break, some people are jogging, others walking, still others reading—and a few napping! The jogging and walking advocates enthusiastically boast of greater energy and happier lives since starting exercising instead of eating at lunch time.

3. Schedule time and places to exercise the laughter muscles. The theatre, movies, stand-up comedians, humorous writers, and television programs all afford opportunities for renewal through laughter. Develop a plan to renew yourself through laughter and follow the plan. By doing so you will enjoy life more and be far more enjoyable at home and work.

4. Take a laughing vacation regularly—a minute, thirty minutes, an evening, or if experiencing too much stress, a few days at a laughing seminar.

In hospitals, therapy groups, educational institutions, and business settings, laughing seminars are conducted. Olive Evans reported the following: "Since 1974 there have been nine national conventions of people including anthropologists and linguists—who are interested in the subject. On April 1, appropriately enough, a five-day International Humor Convention, the sixth, will begin at Arizona State University" (Lexington *Herald-Leader,* Lexington, Kentucky, December 23, 1986).

Laughing is a gift of God to help us live more joyously. It is a form of self-transcendence that causes us to forget ourselves and get in touch with the child in us. George Meredith proclaimed that "Comedy teaches us to look at life exactly as it is, undulled by scientific theories. Comedy banishes 'monstrous monotonousness.' It teaches us to be responsible, to be honest, to interrogate ourselves and correct our pretentiousness."[5]

Robert Short believes that the "Christian faith has been 'let in on' the story of humankind: All humankind is already loved, saved, and redeemed . . . this is why the only truly joyful laughter can come from knowing that there is a happy ending for all people."[6]

Though the following words are surrounded by some harsh ones, the psalmist proclaimed "He who sits in the heavens laughs; the Lord has them in derision" (Psalm 2:4).

Lawrence Peter observed that "we all live in a high-risk neighborhood—the world,"[7] and need the tasteful medicine of laughter to survive.

16

Corporate Worship As Renewal

Do you feel renewed spiritually and emotionally after formal worship? The people answering this question had a wide range of responses. In addition to those who indicated yes or no, or sometimes or seldom, usually or not always, there were the following written comments. See if you can identify your experience in the responses. Remember that the responses are from people representing a cross section of our culture: business executives and assembly line workers, priests and preachers, educators and homemakers, secretaries and surgeons, plumbers and psychiatrists, and many other vocations. The ages of people ranged from twenty-two to seventy-two.

—"I feel renewed, challenged, and upset sometimes after worship service."

—"Sometimes I feel so guilty that I'm not where I should be with God that it overtakes me."

—"I sincerely do. I do not like to miss Sunday A.M. worship."

—"It depends. Sexist language bothers me."

—"I feel renewed during and after."

—"Sometimes. It depends on my frame of mind."

—"Either way up or way down."

—"No! No! No!"

—"Sometimes, if I allow communion with my God throughout."

—"I have so many wishes—I wish the church would *do,* be, understand; sometimes I feel hopeless in the future of the church as a major force in the world."

—"Our entire service gives renewed spirit and faith."

—"No. I am an organist and my husband is the minister."

—"Usually, unless the minister coincidentally preaches on events I have met during the week."

—"Sometimes I am inwardly protesting the minister's theology or grammar."

—"Sometimes I am fighting a feeling of concern for my husband. Is he making a complete idiot of himself, or am I the only one who understands his message?" (spouse of preacher)

—"Usually if I am presiding; occasionally if others are leading."

—"If it is well done."

—"Sometimes. Other times, however, I feel I was there because I was supposed to be there." (clergy spouse)

—"Especially if the music is good."

—"It depends on the quality of the service and how I feel that morning."

—"Especially when I'm an active participant."

—"At times but usually not—only tired and resentful." (clergy)

—"Yes, because I go with the intent of feeling renewed." (clergy)

—"Yes, even when I am in charge and preaching and usually even more so when I have less responsibility for the mechanics." (clergy)

—"Depends on the quality of preparation." (clergy)

—"Yes, as a leader. No and not always when a participant." (clergy)

—"Just relieved that work is over for the day." (clergy)

—"No. I feel it is a performance for me." (clergy)

—"No. Not under present pastor."

—"It depends on what I carry into worship with me and what happens preceding worship."

—"I feel lost if I have to miss worship; my week seems like something is missing."

—"Sometimes perplexed but always uplifted."

—"Sunday worship is the most fun I have all week." (clergy)

—"The combination of fellowship, prayer, music, scripture, communion, and sermons lifts me and helps me face life more effectively the next day and week."

The Importance of Worship

It is obvious that corporate worship is extremely important for many of these people. They attend worship expecting, hoping, and anticipating that they will feel refreshed, re-energized, and renewed when the service is over.

Julia explained, "When I think about church, I think about feeling good. And during the week, when tension builds, conflicts occur, and it feels like the world is closing in on me, I remember that Sunday is not far off. Somehow, I know I will make it. I don't know how people make it without having Sunday worship to look forward to."

Alfred said, "Isn't church fun? I can't wait for Sunday morning to arrive. It charges me for the whole week. After church, I feel like I can handle anything that comes along."

From previous comments we know that not all people are as enthusiastic about worship service as Julia and Alfred are. Many attend worship hoping to be renewed and seldom are. Why are some people renewed and others not? A few factors will be examined.

The Value of Expectancy

Our attitude affects what we receive from worship. The research suggested that people who expected to be renewed usually were. Those who entered worship anticipating a boring or upsetting experience usually found what they looked for.

John Cheever wrote a short story that described the latter person. In it a man attended a party of all beautiful people and spent the entire evening looking for a blemish on someone's face. The worshiper looking for blemishes can usually find a flaw in the sermon, hear an off-key choir member, or find fault with the prayers. If the service is almost flawless, these worshipers can get upset because someone who did not see them did not speak to them. People who refuse to be renewed by worship cannot be renewed.

Renewed in Ritual

There are other factors that affect how people respond to worship. Some people attend worship and are renewed by the ritual. These people are conditioned by a specific ritual to be receptive to God. They are renewed by singing hymns, participating in prayers, the eucharist, hearing the anthems, scripture, and sermons. Change the ritual too much and many of these people have difficulty worshiping. They are disturbed because they did not get the spiritual nourishment needed. They have to hold on for an extra week.

Some people attend worship and may appreciate the worship service, but receive their renewal primarily by being with certain people. They feel alive and joyous singing with, listening to, talking with, and touching and being touched by a handshake or an arm around the shoulder. They feel accepted, appreciated, and know that they "belong." This is their church and these are their people. The church is family. These people are renewed by the same God, but through different means. If fellowship-oriented people's best friends are absent, or if some internationally known clergyperson preaches instead of their preacher, they may not feel renewed. The familiar friendly face in the pulpit makes a difference.

Factors That Affect Us

Other factors affecting people's worship experience:

1. Incidents preceding worship—a family fight on the way to church may not be helpful, and then again worship may help resolve it. The death of a close friend either deepens the religious experience or evokes resentment and anger.

2. The worship service itself may alienate people. If the pastoral prayer or sermon condemns or embarrasses someone, that person probably will not be renewed. If the service appears to beg for more unity because of the lack of preparation, people who have high hopes leave disappointed.

3. Liturgists' feelings while leading worship. Worship leaders communicate what they feel. Because they cannot conceal their feelings, the hostility steams through gritted teeth and by the pretentious smiles. Affection, compassion, and appreciation affect the feelings of parishioners, even when liturgists growl.

4. Relationships with parishioners and pastors. Most people have difficulty worshiping when they are angry with others who are in the worship service. Worship is enhanced by loving relationships. It is extremely difficult for most people to worship if they do not respect the worship leader.

Especially for Leaders

Because some clergy have difficulty being renewed when leading worship the following ideas and suggestions are offered. It is understandable that many clergy (about half of those surveyed) have difficulty being renewed when leading worship, for in addition to the above factors affecting worship there are those peculiar to worship leaders.

Leading worship can be work in a drudgery sense—something I have to do that I do not want to do. When leading worship with this attitude clergy often feel exhausted and resentful. They unconsciously decide that the worship experience is their job, and that part of their job portfolio is to endure the drudgery of leading worship.

Leading worship can be work in a creative, playful sense—an opportunity to lead and participate in a community celebration in which people are renewed. When leading worship with this attitude, clergy often feel exhausted and joyous, or serenely satisfied and rested. They are renewed emotionally and spiritually.

In addition to the previously mentioned factors (personal relationships, incidents immediately preceding worship, and so on) personal preparation seems to influence attitudes toward worship. Clergy who carefully design and mentally rehearse the ritual are more confident and relaxed. Those who wait until Saturday to prepare prayers and sermons usually have to work to conceal the lack of preparation. This produces tension and that tension is communicated to parishioners, and only the determined are renewed by the worship experience. As one man responded to the question about being renewed in formal worship: "Not at church. It bores me to hear the same sermon week in and out." The lack of physical and intellectual preparation affects the worship experience. In such situations clergy are so busy directing the ritual they do not "lose themselves" in worship. Therefore, as in competitive play, if they do a "good job" (win) they are renewed; if not, they are depressed.

Even clergy who prepare and rehearse every detail of the ritual are not always renewed, because they do not prepare themselves emotionally and spiritually. Emotional and spiritual preparation are as important to celebration in worship as intellectual anticipation. Clergy who take time to empathize with the people in the pew and who have some way of making contact with God preceding the service usually "lose themselves" in the service and are renewed.

Is this not also true of all people? To be renewed in

worship, most people need to empathize with people (specific people) and to attempt to make contact with God. With this preparation, which to be helpful must include feelings of love and thanksgiving, people's attitudes enhance the probability of being renewed.

Worship is one way God renews us. Worship proclaims the loving presence of God. In many ways corporate worship offers us renewal through ritual and symbols.

Hymns stir the spirit and tap the memory treasury so that we can remember and proclaim with voice and music our faith in a loving God.

Prayers remind us of our sins—our alienation from some people, our neglect of others, and our need to resolve inner conflicts and other battles that prevent us from becoming the kind of persons we wish others were.

The eucharist assures us of the presence of God in a dramatic way to affirm God's unconditional love as revealed through Jesus Christ.

Scripture weds our today with ancient truth that promises some continuity in the world.

Wisdom from Worship

Sermons may challenge us to "lose ourselves" in a cause worthy of our lives. They may disturb or soothe, depending on people's needs and the preacher's skill and preparation. Worship services offer us forgiveness for the past, hope for the future, and joy for today's living. That is renewing if we are:

1. Trusting enough to turn loose of our vice-grip on our resentments, jealousies, and fears, at least temporarily. Jesus proclaimed a principle when he said, "Forgive us our debts, as we also have forgiven our debtors" (Matthew 6:12). A resentful spirit blocks the experience of love and spontaneous worship.

2. Trusting enough to let things happen to us, instead of trying to make them happen. Instead of deciding what *ought to* happen, be receptive to what does happen. Do not decide ahead of time the criteria for success.

3. Open to and anticipating the awesome presence of God communicating through ritual and people.

4. Accepting of the experiences as our unity and communion with God and others. By accepting our faults and finer characteristics, we present ourselves for renewal. By accepting others' faults and finer characteristics we emotionally and spiritually join the community of faith in forgiveness and faith.

As in play, we recapture the childlikeness that produces a sense of inner harmony, a feeling of union with the universe and God, and the joy that renews. Though this renewing experience does not happen every time, let us pray that it happens often enough to renew us for the celebration of life and loving.

As we can see, the same characteristics required to play playfully are those required to worship spontaneously, and it is the one God renewing us in both experiences.

17

The Presence and Silence of God

Though worship and fellowship with others renew us emotionally and spiritually, they may not resolve the inner conflict and produce the feeling of union with God, and create inner harmony and joy that comes from a mystical experience. Peter Berger thinks the mystical experience is rather rare. He writes, "Whatever the situation may have been in the past, today the supernatural as a meaningful reality is absent or remote from the horizon of everyday."[1]

Andrew Greeley's research indicates the opposite. Greeley concludes that the mystical experience "seems to be reasonably common."

> It involves a breaking away from daily experience of time and place and a search for some sort of basic and primitive union with the Way Things Really Are. While in its origins it was certainly religious, it need not be religious for people today in the sense that it need not have a special

> theological or denominational context. However, in its attempt to come to grips experientially with the Way Things Really Are, the mystical interlude is implicitly and fundamentally religious . . . it is usually triggered by some sort of experience of goodness, truth, beauty, or pleasure that apparently predisposes the person for the mystical event by taking his mind off ordinary events and making him temporarily passive so that "reality may rush in" . . . peace, joy, union, insight, love, confidence, seem to take possession of the person.[2]

People who frequently have mystical experiences are often surprised to discover that all people do not. They assume that the mystical experience is the primary source of hope and the sustaining power that helps people to love others and the "world."

In *The Varieties of Religious Experience,* William James describes the characteristics of the mystical experience. Examine your religious experiences by James's criteria.

The Marks of the Mystical

First, the mystical experience defies explanation. We must experience the mystical event to begin to understand what it means. Then there is not any way to describe it adequately to others. It is a feeling, but more than a feeling.

Second, the mystical experience communicates an understanding of the unity of the universe and one's place in it. We are absolutely sure of this truth. It is a way of knowing that cannot nor need not be validated by anyone or anything else. It is Truth.

Third, the mystical experience comes and goes. It is not a perpetual presence that keeps us on the spiritual mountaintop all day every day. However, once we have a mystical experience our world view, the way we understand and perceive all life, is radically changed. Our faith in and hope for humankind's ultimate welfare is strengthened.

Fourth, the mystical experience cannot be forced. Though we may be able to increase the probability of having a mystical experience, we cannot make it happen. A passive, receptive attitude is necessary.

Fifth, the mystical experience evokes joy and a sense of assurance and faith. The feeling is "all is well" in the ultimate realm of things. We are in touch with something "bigger than life" and we know it. It is a relaxed, receiving, renewing experience; yet, there is more—a new depth to the meaning of life.

Our problems are still present and we deal with them. The mystical experience fortifies us for the daily routine and not-so-routine happenings. While tackling problems, we live *as if* things will eventually be right—maybe not in our lifetime or anybody else's lifetime, but eventually God's love will win out.

Greeley summarizes succinctly Abraham Maslow's "peak experience," which has the distinctive marks of a mystical experience.

> Maslow goes on to say that in peak experiences, the dichotomies, polarities, and conflicts of life are transcended or resolved. There is a loss, though transient, of fear, anxiety, inhibition, of defense and control, of perplexity, confusion, conflict, of delay and restraint. The profound fear of disintegration, of insanity, of death, all tend to disappear for the moment. For Maslow, the peak experience is a "visit to a personally defined heaven from which the person then returns to earth." Upon returning, the person "feels himself more than at other times to be responsible, active, the creative center of his own activities and of his own perceptions, more self-determined, more a free agent, with more free will than at other times."[3]

Jesus said, "You will know the truth, and the truth will make you free" (John 8:32). Is this not the truth, the freedom to become what we were created to be—loving, responsible, interdependent people?

Are Maslow and James writing about something that requires elaborate preparation and exotic, mysterious activities? No. The mystical experience may occur while watching a sunset, or playing with a child, or washing dishes, or listening to music, or making love, or meditating, or praying, or sitting in a church pew, or standing in a church pulpit, or just about any time and any place.

Where Is God?

Yet, there are times when we need and want God's presence to reassure us that at the foundation of creation there is a God who cares. Sometimes, when we think we need God most, it seems that God is on vacation, nowhere to be found. Enticements, promises, and prayers fail to lure God to our side.

Shusaka Endo, the Japanese novelist, captures this feeling of being alone and abandoned by God in his disturbing book, *Silence*. This historical novel is cast during the late sixteenth and early seventeenth centuries when, after years of undisturbed Christian missionary work, the emperor Hideyoshi expelled all Christians from Japan and began persecuting those who remained. Endo graphically describes the ingenuous methods used to make Christians recant their faith. The central character, a priest, asks:

> Why does the song of the exhausted Mokichi, bound to the stake, gnaw constantly at my heart:
>
> We're on our way, we're on our way,
> We're on our way to the temple of Paradise,
> To the temple of Paradise . . .
> To the great Temple . . .
>
> —I have heard from the people of Tomogi that many Christians when dragged off to the place of execution sang this hymn—a melody filled with dark sadness. Life in this world is too painful for these Japanese peasants. Only by relying on "the temple of Paradise" have they been able to go on living. Such is the sadness which fills this song.
>
> —What do I want to say? I myself do not quite understand. Only that today, when for the glory of God Mokichi and Ichizo moaned, suffered and died, I cannot bear the monotonous sound of the dark sea gnawing at the shore. Behind the depressing silence of the sea, the silence of God . . . the feeling that while men raise their voices in anguish, God remains with folded arms, silent.[4]

The great mystics of the church, who devoted their lives to union with God and all that implies, tell of becoming obsessed with the *thought* of God because the spirit of God seemed to be absent. During these periods of doubt, fear, anxiety, guilt, disappointment, and resentment most mystics had a faint hope that God was somewhere and still cared, as Endo's Japanese peasants did.

A Glimmer of Hope

Once people have a mystical experience, thereafter when tragedy occurs which calls one to doubt God, there is usually a glimmer of hope. Shortly before his assassination, Martin Luther King, Jr., preached his famous sermon in which he used the phrase, "I have been to the mountain." King's mystical experience thrust him into the maelstrom of the human rights struggle, and when defeat, disaster, and disappointment tore at his heart and tested his faith, he remembered the mountaintop experience with God and urged others to do so. "We shall overcome" is not just a song about a struggle for human rights by a particular group of people, it is the proclamation of a faith that all people with God's love will overcome the forces that alienate people from people and from God. The struggle for human rights and human dignity continues all over the world and some people get the feeling that while men and women raise their voices in anguish, God remains with folded arms, silent.

The "Silence of God"

Not only is the presence of God through mystical experiences "reasonably common," but the silence of God seems to be also. Ronald, the minister of a small church, and Mary, his spouse, were told that their nine-year-old daughter had leukemia. Ronald, Mary, the members of the congregation, and all their friends prayed for Teresa to be healed. Reverend Ronald assured everyone that God would heal Teresa, although the doctors gave Teresa little hope for recovery. As Teresa's condition deteriorated, Ronald began to feel guilty because he thought that maybe if he had more faith God would make a miracle. Mary felt the loneliness created by Ronald's attitude and by the silence of God. She projected her anger on to Ronald. Finally, Ronald blamed God. Teresa, their only child, died. Ronald and Mary divorced. Ronald loudly pronounced the death of God. He no longer believed in God. He resigned from the church and continued his attack on God. Because of deep depression he sought counseling from a psychologist. After several sessions, the counselor referred Ronald to a pastoral counselor because Ronald's basic problem was the "silence" of God.

Without analyzing this situation in detail, we know that Ronald's belief in and expectations of God were based on God's emergency functions instead of God's presence. This compounded the problems. In their agony, Mary and Ronald could not forget themselves, their personal pain, long enough to hurt with and support each other during the most painful experience loving people can have.

After reading scores of books on theology and talking and listening to the pastoral counselor, Ronald reaffirmed his faith in a loving God, but his specific beliefs in the nature of God and his expectations of God were different. Previous mystical experiences kept the flame of faith faintly flickering while Ronald fought the battle with the silence of God.

Mystical experiences (or if you prefer, peak experiences) renew us whether we encounter them in moments of tragedy or beauty, in play or in prayer, in laughter or in loneliness, because God uses our experience in life to remind us of that holy presence that offers moments of joy.

Thomas Merton, the mystic who refused to leave life alone and things as they were, wrote: ". . . . Futile? Life is not futile if you simply live it. It remains futile, however, as long as you keep watching yourself live it. And that is the old syndrome: Keeping a constant eye on oneself and on one's life, to make sure that the absurd is not showing, that one has company, that one is justified by the presence and support of others."[5]

18

Finding Your Own Way

Arthur Schitzler, the playwright, poet, and novelist, has one of his characters write these words to a friend:

> Man, how I envy you! How the life you are living sparkled and glowed at me from your lines! You understand how to enjoy solitude, and when you gaze into the blue for an hour you get more out of it than people like us get out of a year of wandering in search of adventure. . . . You see, now my one single modest talent, the ability to entertain myself, has been lost. I scrupulously avoid any occasion where it might still be possible—because my last disappointments have soured me. Headaches instead of rapture—that's the hallmark of my whole existence.[1]

In these few words, Schitzler describes two basic approaches to life. One person suffers from seeking constant stimulation only to be disappointed time and time again. He avoids himself by refusing to risk solitude. He has stopped expecting "rapture," because he fears another "headache."

Throughout history there have been those who warned us of busyness—of being so active that we do not stop to find out who we are and where we are headed. In this age of "togetherness" people who want to be alone are viewed as misfits. If you want to be alone many people assume that you must have an emotional problem or be socially maladjusted. Our culture forces and rewards togetherness. "Join the crowd", "Belong to as many organizations as possible", "Make connections", "Be a part of a group", "Keep as busy as possible", "*Do* as much as possible." "If you need anything done, ask a busy person to do it." It works!

The popularity of running probably has as much to do with the fact that it is "alone" time when a person can think and feel and be without constant interruption as it does with the "runner's high" and physical health. Running alone and walking alone are respectable.

The Search for Solitude

Wanting to be alone is viewed with suspicion in our achievement-oriented activistic society. Yet, we know that to be renewed in a deep spiritual and emotional way we need to learn to be in solitude. The Greeks—Aristotle no less than Plato—as well as the great medieval thinkers, held that not only physical, sensuous perception, but equally people's spiritual and intellectual knowledge included an element of pure, receptive contemplation, or as Heraclitus says, of "Listening to the essence of things."[2]

Solitude, contemplation, meditation, suggest not doing instead of doing. That is difficult for those of us who think we have to fix the world and always make sense of everything. Analyze it, explain it, wrap it up in a neat intellectual package so that it can be delivered in a report, or a letter—or a book on play!

It is difficult for people whose minds are racing to capture the key to a problem to turn loose long enough to "let life happen." We know that to be renewed in a deep spiritual and emotional way we need to learn to be in solitude. In solitude we are confronted with our deepest thoughts and darkest desires. There is not anything to distract us, so we may have to come to terms with ourselves. Our pettiness, prejudices, failures, and frivolousness may give us a "headache instead of rapture."

On the other hand, we may be confronted with our kindnesses and compassion, our love and laughter, our hope and happiness. In solitude we may discover that God's grace transcends the headaches and raptures, and embraces all that we are.

The Sound of Silence

Norman Cousins writes, "Silence must be comprehended as not solely the absence of sound. It is the natural environment for serenity and contemplation. Life without silence is life without privacy. The difference between sanity and madness is the quality of our thoughts. Silence is on the side of sanity."[3]

Whether in simple silence, or contemplation, or meditation, or running, or walking, we need some time alone when we can listen without trying to analyze, or explain, or control, or decide what *should* happen.

In *Ash Wednesday,* T. S. Eliot wrote, "Teach us to sit still." Pascal attributed the world's ills to the fact that not enough people were attached to their chairs. In the Old Testament we read, "Be still, and know that I am God" (Psalm 46:10). "The church fathers often spoke of Otium Sanctum: 'Holy leisure.' It refers to a sense of balance in life, an ability to be at peace through the activities of the day, an ability to rest and take time to enjoy beauty, an ability to pace ourselves."[4]

The authors of this book wondered how people paced themselves and if they used specific methods considered "religious" to do so. The question was asked, "*Do you have daily devotionals or some form of meditation?*" The results were interesting. Examine the following to see where you match up.

How People Do It

Many people simply said "no," and a few of these were a little angry that someone would dare pry into their privacy of the holy.

There were people who tried some form of daily devotion or meditation but did not fulfill their resolve to do it regularly. Sporadic was the word most often used to describe their behavior.

"I used to. An hour divided mostly between prayer and Bible study. Really essential for my well-being."

"Sometimes for months I am disciplined in this way; sometimes for months I slip away from intentional devotional life."

"I've started it each morning a thousand times, but I cannot consistently get up early enough to do it."

These confessions remind us of the following: "The people I've met who say they 'used' to fish can never give a good account of why they stopped. Neither can they explain the meaning of their existence."

In the Grip of Guilt

Many people feel guilty for not having a regular period and methods for devotionals or meditation. They think they *ought to.* They *ought to* have devotionals and they *ought to* like to spend an hour in meditation. Because the meditation time does not feel urgent, it gets bumped from the schedule when it is needed most—when they are the busiest. Another thing causing sporadic behavior is that some people *think* they ought to use this method of being with God, but do not *feel* comfortable with the practice. Some are bored, others feel handcuffed. Though the following may sound like an attack on the sacred, some people do not benefit from daily devotions or structured meditation. When "forced," instead of creating communion with God it causes resentment toward God. It does not renew, it creates more tension in these people.

Donald explained, "I do not consider myself a pious person, nor does regular, disciplined or scheduled devotions and meditation appeal to me. I don't feel guilty about this because I receive throughout the daily pilgrimage the still small voice of God's presence, even when I am woodcarving which is my main play activity."

Sherman wrote, "I've never been comfortable with the notion of 'daily devotionals.' I think I regard the term itself, or the idea underlying it, as coercive. So, I do not have an established pattern or habit of meditation. Each day, however, finds me spontaneously doing some reflective thinking about myself, my loved ones, my faith and church, and about the human family and the problems it has itself up against."

Thomas Langford wrote, "A thing worth doing is worth doing with joy." When a particular practice of trying to commune with God does not occasionally pay off with joy, the practice is abandoned. Daily devotions, meditations, and prayers are not going to produce ecstatic experiences or serene moments every time, but if occasionally we don't feel a little lift instead of disappointment, we will find other ways to use our time.

There are those who avoid structured spiritual exercises because they grew up hearing preachers and teachers, in all good consciousness and with good intentions, defame God's character. In his autobiography, Jean Paul Sartre, the French existentialist, wrote, "I did not recognize in the fashionable God in whom I was taught to believe the one whom my soul was awaiting. I needed a Creator; I was given a Big Boss." Only masochists want to spend time with an insensitive, dictatorial Big Boss who will not listen except to learn how to keep them under control.

Devotional Methods

Hundreds of people gladly shared their methods of being renewed through daily devotions or some form of meditation. Following are some of their comments:

"I take the time to be alone with myself and my

thoughts. I generally first deal in my mind with what is going on around me and then pray and read a psalm."

"There is not scheduled time, but I take time usually during simple tasks to meditate."

"Three times a day I read the Bible and a devotional."

"Daily I use the ACTS to start the day. ***A***doration (psalm or praise song) just to be in God's presence, ***C***onfession, ***T***hanksgiving for blessings, ***S***upplication for my and other's needs."

"Morning quiet time. Mass as often as possible at noon."

"Meditation, rosary devotion, spiritual reading, holy Mass."

"Read scripture, quiet time and tend to let my mind float."

"We pray together as a community (five members) in the morning and evening and I have a daily meditation of thirty minutes to an hour daily."

"Meditate on the experiences of the day and my relationship with those I encounter."

"Before going to sleep, I leave myself open to listen to God, with perhaps a short prayer."

"Every morning before I rise I pray and mention by name every person on my prayer list, then have a talk with God."

"I pray at work, sing, and think of God's goodness."

"Usually a few minutes before the alarm rings, I thank God for what I've got and ask help for the day."

"I center myself through breathing exercises and then open myself to receive God's presence."

"While running I communicate with and in nature."

"I find time to be alone, to walk, to sit under a tree or whatever, and to relax into the presence of God in the world."

Practicing the Presence

Some form of meditation or regular private devotional seems to be essential for some people's emotional and spiritual well-being. Those who practice daily communion with God in some form derive much satisfaction and support from it.

For those who want to establish a consistent practice of some form of meditation or communion with God there is hope. The first thing to realize is that there is not a right and wrong way nor a right or wrong time. The second thing to realize is that God will commune with us on our territory. If walking, or bathing in a warm tub of water, or washing the dishes is a receptive time for you, try it; others have. If poetry or scripture creates a feeling of openness, one of these may work for you. In his excellent book, *Celebration of Discipline: The Path to Spiritual Growth,* Richard Foster writes, "God has given us the Disciplines of the spiritual life as a means of receiving His grace. The Disciplines allow us to place ourselves before God so that he can transform us . . . the way of disciplined grace . . . it is 'grace' because it is free; it is disciplined because there is something for us to do."[5]

The third thing to realize is that our attitude, openness, and expectations have everything to do with whether or not we are renewed by prayer and meditation. God is not primarily a compassionate clerk to whom we present our checklist of wants and then check out of the conversation. (Though our checklist does reveal our values.) God is primarily a presence who makes a difference in us and between us and others, much as a good friend does, only more so. A friend is someone who listens to us caringly, criticizes us when we are doing something that hurts us, and who loves us even when we are not very lovable. It is who we are when we are with a friend that enables us to relax and become more than we thought we could be. The friend's presence makes a difference to us, in us, and between us and others.

The Difference It Makes

It is God's presence that makes a difference to us, in us, and between us and others, not the checklist of wants.

Because we experience that presence as creating worth in us by loving us, we can manage most of the checklist ourselves. When we experience God's love, we understand Matthew Fox's description of prayer: "Prayer is not a substance to be isolated any more than people are; it is a process, an attitude of falling even more deeply in love with life."[6] We may even understand Moltmann's words, "When we cease using God as helper in need, stop gap, and problem-solver, we are—according to the Augustine—finally free for . . . the joy of God and the enjoyment of each other in God."[7]

We find our way to commune with and be renewed by God. Most of us do not have great peak experiences and dramatic religious conversions. We just want to make it day by day and to know that God and a few friends are with us. To do so we need what Maslow calls plateau experiences. Consider his words: "The less intense plateau experience is more often experienced as pure enjoyment and happiness, as, let's say, in a mother sitting quietly looking by the hour at her baby playing, and marveling, wondering, philosophizing, not quite believing. She can experience this as a very pleasant, continuing, contemplative experience rather than as something akin to a climactic explosion which then ends."[8]

The plateau experience renews us emotionally and spiritually whether playing or praying; this is, if we are not too busy to notice. Some people's play is their meditation. Other people's meditation is their play. Whenever and however the experience with God occurs then "we know and believe the love God has for us. God is love, and he who abides in love abides in God, and God abides in him" (1 John 4:16).

10

Action Follows Being

Bemoaning the fact that life is too short, Kurt Vonnegut wrote, "I was born only yesterday morning, moments after daybreak—and yet, this afternoon, I am fifty-four years old. I am a mere baby, and yet here I am dedicating a library. Something has gone wrong."[1]

Feeling as though life has passed them by in a flash is a common experience of people who stay too busy collecting trophies of achievement to notice and appreciate the sacred art of life as it is revealed in friendships, families, children, sunsets, music, work, and worship. This book has stressed the need to live the rhythm of life God created—to work and play, to learn and love, to worship and be renewed by being in touch with the deeper dimensions of our created nature.

The theologian Paul Tillich captured the thought when he wrote:

> We call Jesus the Christ not because He brought a new religion but because He is the end of religion, above religion and irreligion, above Christianity and

> non-Christianity. We spread His call because it is the call to every [person] in every period to receive the New Being, that hidden saving power in our existence, which takes from us labor and burden, and gives rest to our souls.
>
> Do not ask in this moment what we shall do or how action shall follow from the New Being, from the rest in our souls. Do not ask; for you do not ask how the good fruits follow from the goodness of a tree. They follow; action follows being, and new action, better action, stronger action follows new being, better being, stronger being. We and our world would be better, truer, and more just, if there were more rest for our souls in the world. Our actions would be more creative, more conquering, conquering the tragedy of our time, if they grew out of a more profound level of our life. For our creative depth is the depth in which we are quiet.[2]

In 1985 while Loren visited church leaders in the Philippines, he witnessed this phenomenon Tillich described. In the midst of political oppression, poverty, and assassinations, Filipino Christians took time to celebrate their faith and friendship. Knowing that at any moment they might be arrested or killed for speaking out for people in poverty or for clergy in prison, they criticized those in political power. They were trying to save their part of the world by seeking medical aid for the forgotten masses who would never see a physician, food for children who will suffer brain damage from malnutrition, and homes for families whose parents had been assassinated. Under these oppressive conditions, some Filipino Christians took time to celebrate in festivals, friendships, and worship while proclaiming in word and deed the love of God.

These people have discovered that to keep up the struggle, they have to take time to rest their souls. They know that to maintain hope in their Christian cause, and strength and courage for the struggle they must draw upon the Truth of God's liberating spirit within themselves and between themselves and others. "Action follows being, and new action, better action, stronger action follows new being, better being, stronger being."

One is reminded of Jesus' words, "Whoever would

save his life will lose it, and whoever loses his life for my sake will find it" (Matthew 16:25). These words are embodied by the Reverend Gloria Guzman, a Filipino Christian, who lives with a joy in her heart, laughter and prophecy on her lips, and a compassion big enough to encompass the whole world. Another theologian, Rosemary Radford Ruether, described Gloria Guzman and many other Filipino Christians when she wrote, "The essence of servanthood is that it is possible only for liberated persons, not people in servitude. Also it exercises power and leadership, but in a new way, not to reduce others to dependency, but to empower and liberate others."[3]

Whether in play, prayer, creative work, or inspiring worship, when we experience the Truth revealed through our creative depth we think more clearly, have more energy, and act more responsibly. We do so because we temporarily break through the enculturating crust of pride, prejudices, fears, frustrations, guilt, and greed, that prevent us from experiencing the liberating spirit of God.

The creative depth of which Tillich writes is the Truth of our created nature which reveals:

1. That it is possible to turn fear into faith, guilt into grace, and compulsive competitiveness into compassion for the enemy;

2. That we are free to try both to enjoy and save the world—to create with God a world in which all people are treated with dignity and respect;

3. That we are a vital part of creation and are in mysterious ways related to all people and living things;

4. That we are global citizens dependent upon one another for physical, emotional, intellectual, and spiritual growth; and

5. That we have reason to hope for a just and peaceful world in which love will eventually overcome evil.

As Christians and other people of good will, living what we believe is difficult under the best of circumstances; it is almost impossible to do so with a joyous spirit if we do not take time to be renewed intellectually, emotionally, and spiritually.

Seminar on Play

This sign appears over a plant manager's office door: "If you have problems, come in and tell me about them. If you don't, come in and tell me how you do it." As the sign suggests, the difference in people is not in those who have problems and those who don't. All people have problems. It is the type of problems that makes the differences. Another difference between people is how they perceive problems. Some people see problems as persistent irritants to be endured—terrible things to live with and through. These people say such things as, "I don't know how to play. I'm impatient and highstrung. That's just the way I am." They do not believe they can change. They feel doomed to live as they always have.

Other people see problems as challenges to be conquered. They say such things as, "I don't know how to play, but I am going to learn." Changing the way we live and feel is difficult. Discovering that we do not have to be compulsive competitors or workaholics does not automatically relieve us of the stressful feelings and destructive behavior. It is so because in compulsive competitiveness, work habits, play, and prayer we are not just dealing with thoughts. We are dealing with attitudes, which include deeply ingrained thoughts, feelings, and behavior. When dealing with such complex issues, studying and sharing with others is an effective way to turn problems into challenges to be conquered.

The following principles and procedures for conducting seminars on play have been used to help many people discover a more joyous way of living.

Atmosphere for Change

The seminars should be designed to create an atmosphere of Christian community in which people may "tell it like it is" instead of pretending life is as it should be. Ideally, the seminar will include the following. People will become comfortable enough with each other to talk about their problems. They must trust others to listen to their story without fear of ridicule. This is not to suggest that people will be coerced into telling secrets. People should not feel as though they have to confess anything. They should feel free to discuss ideas, express feelings, and experiment with behavior.

If trust, acceptance, and openness develop between participants in the seminar, laughter will be a part of every session. Participants will discover and enjoy the humor in human behavior. When they begin to laugh at themselves and with others, they will be free to accept and to change their unwanted behavior and hurtful feelings. They may even discover that God works through people to help them accept themselves as they are so they can become more than they thought they could be.

Procedures for Seminars

1. After explaining what can be expected from the seminar and introducing the topic for study, each session

should suggest that participants tell something about themselves. This enables participants to feel a part of the group and affirms their right to talk and listen.

The topics from the questionnaire on pages 19 and 20 of this book are one way this may be accomplished. The first session may begin with participants stating their name and responding to "Do you take time to play? If so, how much time?" Or participants may be asked to state their name and hobbies.

2. In the first session, have the participants fill out the questionnaire on pages 19 and 20. Answers to the questions become the basis for designing the specific content of the seminars. It is important for participants to believe that their interest will be addressed.

3. Because people usually speak more openly in small groups, each session should include time for discussion in subgroups of three to five people. This increases the probability of all participants having the opportunity to deal with their specific problems and to feel supported by others while they try to solve problems.

4. Ninety minutes is usually the most productive time frame. This gives time for minilectures, discussion in the total group, and subgroups.

5. Assign chapters of this book to be read before the following meeting. This gives participants a common experience and may keep them conscious of what they are trying to do.

6. Suggest that participants choose activities they will complete before the next seminar session. This may include keeping a time log, playing with the children, spouse, or friend, or praying at a specific time each day. Arranging for people to tell their intentions to others is usually helpful, because they are then accountable to themselves publicly.

7. Encourage participants to tell how they fulfilled their intention the previous week, "What did you say you were going to do? Did you do it?" This is usually a fun time of sharing.

Sample Seminar Design

Seminars are planned for specific people and should reflect their interests and needs. In some settings, the major emphasis may be on play; in another setting the people may be more receptive to a prayer emphasis. In a setting where scores of people have lost their jobs, the seminar may focus on the dignity of work and play. The following six sessions illustrate one method for designing a seminar, which could serve as a prelude to other programs. Sections of the book on procrastination, worship, and prayer each could be the themes for four to eight session seminars.

The sessions described herein are tightly structured. The leader should be flexible enough to add or delete material as the people's interest and needs emerge.

Session One

7:00 Introduction of Seminar
The introduction and chapter 1 can be used for this introduction.

7:15 Participants state their name and describe their hobbies and tell how often they enjoy them.

7:25 Participants fill out the "Play and Worship" questionnaire.
Reproduce the questionnaire from the book for this activity.

7:35 Participants divide into groups of three to five people and share their responses to the questionnaire.

7:55 A representative from each group reports the responses to the total group. Discussion follows.

8:10 Questionnaires are given to the leader. The leader explains that the seminar will be adjusted to meet the interest and needs of the participants.

8:15 Participants choose an activity they will try to do before the next meeting and tell it to the person sitting next to them.

8:20 Assign chapters 1, 2, and 3 for the next session.

8:25 Participants describe in one or two words how they feel about the seminar.
Closing prayer.

Session Two

7:00 Participants state name and describe an activity they enjoyed the past week. "Did you feel renewed?"
7:10 Lecture—Review the contents of chapter 2, followed by a discussion of definitions of play and leisure. List definitions on newsprint for discussion.
7:25 Discuss—Can you play? Do you play enough?
7:45 Lecture—Review phase I of burnout.
7:55 In subgroups, participants discuss personal experiences of burnout and/or the use and misuse of play time.
8:15 Representatives of each group report to total group.
8:25 Ask participants to use the steps suggested in "A Constructive Use of Frustration" (chapter 3).
Participants state the activity they planned for the previous week and report the results of their good intentions.
8:30 Assign chapter 4 for next session.
Closing prayer.

Session Three

7:00 Participants report on the use of the frustration steps.
(They should know each other's names by this time.)
7:15 Lecture—Review phases II and III of burnout, emphasizing the questions on pages 31 and 32, followed by a discussion in the total group.
7:40 Lecture—Describe "Losing Ourselves in Play," using Kelty's description of rapture and Maslow's peak experiences.
7:50 In subgroups, participants discuss concepts and share experiences of "losing themselves" in play.

"Have you had a peak experience or an experience of rapture?"

8:15 Representatives from subgroups share groups' responses and raise questions for discussion.

8:30 Assign chapters 5, 6, and 7.
Participants choose an activity to complete before the next session and tell someone what it is.
Closing prayer.

Session Four

7:00 Participants answer the question, "Can you do nothing? (that is, just relax and 'let the world go by')? If so, how and where do you do it?"

7:15 Lecture—Review ideas in chapters 6 and 7, stressing the various relationships between work, play, and competition.

7:30 In subgroups, participants discuss the ideas from the lecture.
Possible thought starters are: "Is everything competition for you?"; "Do you believe in the Protestant work ethic?"; "What message about work and play do you remember from childhood?"

8:00 Representatives from subgroups report to the total group.

8:15 Open discussion.

8:25 Assign chapters 8 and 9.
Participants report on their success or failure with the activity they chose to do the previous week.
Participants choose an activity for the following week and tell someone what it is.
Closing prayer.

Session Five

7:00 Participants respond to: "Do you feel guilty when you play?"

7:10 Lecture—Introduce the subject of guilt-feelings by listing and reviewing the quotes on page 57.

7:20 Open discussion.
7:30 Participants list all things and people who make them feel guilty.
7:40 In subgroups, "talk about those issues you don't mind sharing and note who (or what) taught you to feel guilty about them."
8:00 Representatives from subgroups share group's responses with the total group.
8:10 Lecture on "Guilt, Grace, and God" (chapter 9).
8:25 Participants report on last week's personal activity. Participants choose an activity to complete before the next session and tell someone what it is.
Assign chapters 14 and 16.
Closing prayer.

Session Six

7:00 List on chalkboard or newsprint the characteristics of play described on pages 99 and 100. After reviewing the characteristics, ask participants, "Does this describe your play?
Are you renewed emotionally and spiritually in the way described by the characteristics of play?"
7:20 Lecture on "Those who humble themselves like a child"—pages 101, 102, and 103.
7:30 In subgroups, participants discuss, "Do you feel renewed spiritually and emotionally after formal worship? If so, what part of the worship experience helps you the most? Ritual? Friend? Other?"
8:00 Lecture and discussion on "getting the most out of formal worship," chapter 16.
8:20 Participants report on the previous week's personal activity.
8:30 Evaluation—Have participants respond in writing to the following and give responses to the leader.
1. List three things about the seminar that were helpful to you.
2. List three ways the seminar can be improved.
3. Would you participate in a similar seminar again?

4. Do you want to continue this study? If so, note the subjects you want to study.

Closing prayer.

Final Note

If the participants experienced Christian community, they will want and need to have a special celebration—a party, a special worship service, or both.

Endnotes

Introduction

1. For some of the most insightful, interesting, and entertaining reading found anywhere, see: *Letters of E.B. White* (New York: Harper and Row, 1976) and *Essays of E.B. White* (New York: Harper and Row, 1977).

Chapter 1

1. Adapted from Lois A. Cheney, *God Is No Fool* (Nashville: Abingdon Press, 1969).
2. Meyer Friedman and Ray H. Rosenman, *Type A Behavior and Your Heart* (New York: Alfred Knopf, 1974).
3. Conrad Hyers, *The Comic Vision and the Christian Faith* (New York: Pilgrim Press, 1981) 38.

Chapter 4

1. Matthew Kelty, *Sermons in a Monastery* (Kalamazoo: Cistercian Publications, 1983) 39.
2. Abraham H. Maslow, *The Farther Reaches of Human Nature* (New York: Viking Press, 1971) 178.

Chapter 6

1. Arnold Toynbee, "Why and How I Work," *Saturday Review*, April 1969.

2. Roberta J. Park, "Too Important to Trust to the Children: In Search for Freedom and Order in Children's Play, 1900–1917" in *Paradoxes of Play*, editor John Loy (West Point: Leisure Press, 1982) 101, 102.

3. For an interesting interpretation of indulgences, see: Kenneth Latourette, *A History of Christianity* (New York: Harper and Row, 1953).

4. Charles F. Kemp, *A World of Golf and the Game of Life* (St. Louis: Bethany Press, 1978) 26.

5. Robert K. Johnston, *The Christian at Play* (Grand Rapids: Wm. B. Eerdmans Publishing Company, 1983) 16.

6. Robert Neale, *In Praise of Play* (New York: Harper and Row, 1969) 13.

Chapter 7

1. Jürgen Moltmann, *Theology of Play* (New York: Harper and Row, 1971) 64.

2. Richard N. Bolles, *The Three Boxes of Life* (Berkley: Ten Speed Press, 1978) 354.

3. Robert K. Johnston, 8.

4. Norman Cousins, *Human Options* (New York: W. W. Norton, 1981) 69.

5. Josef Pieper, *Leisure: The Basis of Culture.* Tr: Alexander DRV (New York: The New American Library, 1952) 43.

6. Robert Neale, 36, 38.

7. Quoted in *Lost in the Cosmos—The Last Self-Help Book,* Walter Percy (New York: Washington Square Press, 1983) 179.

Chapter 8

1. Woody Allen, *Side Effects* (New York: Ballantine Books, 1975) 15.

2. Paul Tournier, *Guilt and Grace* (New York: Harper and Row, 1958) 135.

3. Willard Gaylin, *Caring* (New York: Avon Books, 1976) 125.

Chapter 9

1. Paul Tournier, *Guilt and Grace* (New York: Harper and Row, 1958) 150.

2. For an additional study of these themes on love, see *The Walls Can Fall* by Catherine and Loren Broadus (St. Louis: Christian Board of Publication, 1985).

3. Thomas C. Oden, *Game Free: A Guide to the Meaning of Intimacy* (New York: Harper and Row, 1974).
4. Paul Tournier, 129.
5. Robert K. Johnston, 44.

Chapter 10

1. Loren Broadus, *How to Stop Procrastinating and Start Living* (Minneapolis: Augsburg Press, 1983).

Chapter 11

1. Graham Greene, *A Sort of Life* (New York: Washington Square Press, 1971) 137.
2. *Encyclopedia of Psychology.* 1982 edition. "Boredom," G. D. Wilson.
3. Woody Allen, 81.
4. Kenneth Blanchard and Spencer Johnson, *The One Minute Manager* (New York: Berkley Books, 1982).
5. David Conover, *One Man's Island* (New York: Crown Publishing, 1971) 8.
6. Quoted in "The Curse of Leisure Time" by Judi Balley, *Kiwanis Quarterly,* May 1983.
7. Paul Tournier, *Learn to Grow Old* (New York: Harper and Row, 1972) 5.
8. Richard N. Bolles, 335.
9. Judi Balley, *The Curse of Leisure Time* (Kiwanis Magazine, May, 1983).

Chapter 12

1. Johan Huizinger, *Homo Ludens* (Boston: Beacon Press, 1950) Foreword.
2. For an exposition of this theme, see: Richard C. Gillett, "The Reshaping of Work: A Challenge to the Churches," *The Christian Century,* January 5–12, 1983.
3. Robert E. Neale, 24.
4. A friend mailed this quote to the authors. Source unknown.
5. Dan Kiley, *The Peter Pan Syndrome* (New York: Dodd, Mead and Company, 1983) 22, 24.
6. William Paulsell, *Letters from a Hermit* (Springfield: Templegate Publishers, 1978) 13.

Chapter 13

1. *Esquire,* February 1985.
2. Norman Cousins, 32.

3. Charles Swindoll, "Busyness," *Ministry,* November 1983.
4. George Sheehan, *The Running of Life* (New York: Simon and Schuster, 1980) 141.

Chapter 14

1. Wayne Oates, *Confessions of a Workaholic* (New York: World Publishing, 1971) 8.

Chapter 15

1. Norman Cousins, *Anatomy of an Illness* (New York: W. W. Norton & Co., 1979).
2. Wylie Sypher, *Comedy* (Garden City: Doubleday Anchor Books, 1956) 241.
3. Jürgen Moltmann, *Theology of Play* (New York: Harper and Row, 1971) 13.
4. Milan Kundera, *The Book of Laughter and Forgetting*. Tr: Michael Henry Heim (New York: Penguin Books, 1981) 56.
5. Wylie Sypher, 9.
6. Robert Short, *Something to Believe In* (New York: Harper and Row, 1978).
7. Lawrence J. Peter and Bill Dana, *The Laughter Prescription* (New York: Ballantine Books, 1982).

Chapter 17

1. Peter L. Berger, *Rumors of Angels* (Garden City: Doubleday and Company, 1966) 7.
2. Andrew M. Greeley, *Ecstasy—A Way of Knowing* (Englewood Cliffs: Prentice-Hall, 1974) 47, 48.
3. Ibid, 20.
4. Shusaku Endo, *Silence.* Tr: William Johnston (Tokyo: Kodansha International, 1966) 105.
5. Quoted in Michael Mott, *The Seven Mountains of Thomas Merton* (Boston: Houghton Mifflin Company, 1984) 335.

Chapter 18

1. Arthur Schitzler, *The Little Comedy and Other Stories* (New York: Frederick Ungar Publishers, 1977) 1, 2.
2. Joseph Pieper, 26.
3. Norman Cousins, 68.
4. Richard J. Foster, *Celebration of Discipline: The Path to Spiritual Growth* (San Francisco: Harper and Row, 1978) 20, 21.
5. Ibid, 6.

6. Matthew Fox, *On Becoming a Musical Mystical Bear* (New York: Paulist Press, 1972) 14.

7. Jürgen Moltmann, 63.

8. Abraham H. Maslow, *Religions, Values, and Peak Experiences* (New York: Viking Press, 1964) 15.

Chapter 19

1. Kurt Vonnegut, *Palm Sunday* (New York: Dell Publishing Company, Inc., 1981) 157–158.

2. Paul Tillich, *The Shaking of the Foundations* (New York: Charles Scribner's Sons, 1948) 102–103.

3. Rosemary Radford Ruether, *To Change the World—Christology and Cultural Criticism* (New York: Crossroad, 1981) 54.

CATHERINE and LOREN BROADUS are the authors of *Laughing and Crying with Little League* (Harper and Row), *From Loneliness to Intimacy* (John Knox), and *The Walls Can Fall* (Christian Board of Publication). Loren also wrote *How to Stop Procrastinating and Start Living* (Augsburg). The Broaduses make their home in Lexington, Kentucky, where Loren is professor of ministerial practice at Lexington Theological Seminary. They are actively involved in conducting seminars on play, out of which activity this book developed. They are the parents of three sons.